Detroit TIGERS TRIVIA

JOHN F. GRABOWSKI

Quinlan Press
Boston

Copyright © 1988
by John F. Grabowski
All rights reserved,
including the right of reproduction
in whole or in part in any form.
Published by Quinlan Press
131 Beverly Street
Boston, MA 02114

Cover design by Lawrence Curcio
Cover photo by David C. Coates,
 The Detroit News
Inside photos courtesy of the National
Baseball Library, Cooperstown, New York

Library of Congress
Catalog Card Number 87-63334
ISBN 1-55770-015-X

Printed in the United States of America
May 1988

To Trish and Elizabeth, and my other Mom.

I would like to thank the public relations department of the Detroit Tigers, Ernie Harwell, and Mike Getz for their assistance.

John F. Grabowski was educated at the City College of New York, where he was a member of the baseball team, and at Teacher's College, Columbia University, where he received his Masters in Educational Psychology. He currently teaches high school math and computer studies on Staten Island. When he is not teaching, he is a free-lance writer who has had several hundred pieces published in newspapers, magazines and the programs of professional sports teams. The author of *Super Sports Word Find Puzzles, Dodgers Trivia, Cleveland Browns Trivia* and *San Francisco 49ers Trivia,* he has also been the publisher and editor of the monthly *Baseball Trivia Newsletter*. A nationally syndicated columnist, his weekly "Stat Sheet" is supplied to over 600 newspapers by N.E.A.

Contents

History
  Questions 1
  Answers 17
Post-Season Play
  Questions 29
  Answers 49
At the Plate and on the Bases
  Questions 61
  Answers 71
The Brain Trust
  Questions 77
  Answers 85
The Battery
  Questions 91
  Answers 107
The Infield
  Questions 117
  Answers 125
The Outfield
  Questions 129
  Answers 135
Records and Firsts
  Questions 139
  Answers 151
Photographs
  Questions 159
  Answers 169
Miscellaneous
  Questions 171
  Answers 185

History

1. What was the first home field of the Detroit Tigers?

2. Who was the park named for?

3. What was unusual about the layout of the park?

4. Can you name the hurler who won the first game ever played by the Tigers?

5. How did Detroit win the game?

6. Who drove in the winning run that first game?

7. What major league record did Pop Dillon set in that initial contest?

8. Who was the Tigers' first field manager?

History — Questions

9. Who was the only Detroit regular to hit .300 that first season?

10. Following continual disagreements with his star outfielder, manager Hughie Jennings reportedly offered Ty Cobb to the Cleveland Indians in 1907 in exchange for a veteran outfielder. Who was this future Hall-of-Famer?

11. Name the Tiger pitcher who posted a 25-4 mark in 1907, for a league-leading .862 winning percentage.

12. How many players appeared in a Detroit uniform in the Tigers' pennant-winning season of 1907?

13. In 1908, a ten-year-old black orphan became the batboy/mascot/good luck charm of the Tigers, and Ty Cobb in particular. What was his name?

14. Tiger Stadium was officially opened on April 20, 1912. What other American League stadium first opened its doors that same day?

15. On May 18, 1912, the Tiger players walked out in protest over a suspension handed out to Ty Cobb for going into the stands after a fan. In order to avoid a $5,000 fine, manager Jennings

History — Questions

rounded up a group of St. Joseph's College (Philadelphia) players for the game against Philadelphia. Who was the 20-year old student who pitched for Detroit?

16. What line of work did he eventually go into when his brief major league career was over?

17. What was the result of the game?

18. How did Ed Irvin perform that day?

19. Which of the replacement players later appeared in one game for the Phillies, in 1916, and was reputed to be a "go-between" in the 1919 World Series thrown by the "Black Sox"?

20. Which replacement player wore Ty Cobb's uniform?

21. Deacon McGuire closed out his major league career with his appearance in the game. How many seasons did he play in the big time?

22. In the war-shortened 1918 season, Bobby Veach led the American League in runs batted in. How many did he collect?

History — Questions

23. The 1921 Tigers set the AL season mark for team batting with a .316 average. Can you name the eight regulars on that club?

24. Who were the only regulars to fail to hit .300 that season?

25. Where did Detroit finish in the standings that year?

26. This Hall of Fame hurler was given a tryout by Detroit in the spring of 1926, but did not impress manager Ty Cobb, who ordered him not to throw his "freak" pitch because it would ruin his arm. Can you name this future Giant mainstay?

27. Name the Detroit first baseman who turned an unassisted triple play in a 1927 game against Cleveland.

28. Which Tiger catcher of the late 1920s had a brother who was a catcher in the National League?

29. How did Charlie Gehringer perform on "Charlie Gehringer Day" in 1929?

30. This first baseman began the 1932 season with Detroit, and was dealt to

History — Questions

Boston on June 12. He went on to lead the American League in batting —the only player ever to do so while dividing a season between two teams. Can you name him?

31. Under the current major league rule, would this player have won the batting title in 1932?

32. Mickey Cochrane came to the Tigers in a December 1933 trade with Philadelphia. Who did the Athletics receive in the deal?

33. Who did Detroit send to Washington in order to obtain Goose Goslin in 1933?

34. Who did the Bengals obtain from the Browns in 1936 to take the place of Hank Greenberg, who had broken his wrist 12 games into the season?

35. How was Mickey Cochrane's major league career ended?

36. Who entered the game to replace Cochrane after his injury?

37. For what other piece of baseball trivia is Bump Hadley remembered?

History — Questions

38. Navin Field was remodeled, and its seating capacity expanded from 36,000 to 56,000 in time for the 1938 season. What other change was made?

39. Detroit won the last game of the 1938 season in spite of an outstanding performance by the opposing Cleveland pitcher. Who was he and what did he do?

40. Who won the game for Detroit?

41. Detroit and St. Louis pulled off a ten-player deal in May of 1939. How many of the principals involved can you name?

42. What was the result of the Tigers' first night game?

43. When and where was it played?

44. The 1939 squad terminated significant winning streaks—one of 12 games, and one of 11—for two pitchers. Can you name the hurlers who saw their skeins ended by the Bengals?

45. Who did the Tigers obtain from the Cubs in a 1940 trade of shortstops?

History — Questions

46. Which "unknown" pitcher clinched the 1940 pennant for the Tigers by beating Bob Feller and the Indians in a late-season game?

47. The manager of the Indians that day was a former Tiger. Name him.

48. How many more major league games did the "unknown" pitcher win after the clincher?

49. Who did Detroit obtain to replace Hank Greenberg, who entered the service in 1941?

50. The Tigers signed outfielder Dick Wakefield for a reported $52,000 bonus in 1941. Which school had Wakefield played for?

51. To whom did the Tigers sell Schoolboy Rowe in April of 1942?

52. Due to a ruling by Commissioner Kenesaw Mountain Landis, all major league teams were required to train at northern sites in 1943. Where did the Tigers set up camp?

53. Which five Tigers joined the armed forces in 1943?

History — Questions

54. Which five Tigers joined the armed forces in 1944?

55. Which year was the first that the Tigers did not have a starting player voted to the American League All-Star team?

56. Which two Detroit pitchers finished 1-2 in the AL in earned run average in 1944?

57. Which two hurlers duplicated the feat the next year?

58. Two Detroit players missed large chunks of the 1946 season after colliding with each other during a game. Name them.

59. Who did the Tigers send to Philadelphia in exchange for third baseman George Kell in 1946?

60. How did the Tigers fare in the first night game ever played in Detroit?

61. When did it take place?

62. Name the Detroit pitcher who was seriously injured in 1949 in a spring training auto accident?

History — Questions

63. What was unusual about Detroit's 10-9 victory over New York on June 23, 1950?

64. How many homers were hit in the game?

65. Which two Detroit pitchers entered military service in 1951?

66. The 1951 All-Star game was originally scheduled for Philadelphia. Why was it switched to Detroit?

67. At what school did Harvey Kuenn play ball, prior to joining the Tigers in 1952?

68. In June of 1952, the Tigers and Red Sox completed a nine-player deal. Who were the players involved?

69. What ignominious feat did the 1952 Tigers accomplish?

70. Who were the three "bonus babies" signed by the Tigers in 1953?

71. Which Hall-of-Famer teamed with Van Patrick to broadcast Tigers games in the mid-1950s?

History — Questions

72. What do Bill Veeck, Jack Kent Cooke and Charley Finley have in common?

73. The Tigers had two 20-game winners on their staff in 1956. Who were they?

74. In what position did the team finish that season?

75. In 1957, the Tigers and Athletics completed a 13-player deal. How many of the players involved can you name?

76. Harvey Kuenn shifted from shortstop to center field in 1958. Which future Tiger manager took his place in the infield?

77. What tragedy befell the Tigers' family in November of 1958?

78. Which two former Cleveland relief stars came to Detroit in the same deal in November of 1958?

79. Which Hall of Fame broadcaster began announcing for the Tigers in 1960?

80. On Opening Day in 1960, Detroit defeated Cleveland in the longest season-opener ever. Who was the winning pitcher in the 15-inning affair?

History — Questions

81. Who did the Tigers send to Cleveland in exchange for home run champ Rocky Colavito in April of 1960?

82. Which players did the Tigers lose to the Los Angeles Angels in the 1960 expansion draft?

83. Which players did the Tigers lose to the Washington Senators in the 1960 expansion draft?

84. Who did Detroit send to Cleveland in exchange for Norm Cash in 1960?

85. When did Briggs Stadium officially have its name changed to Tiger Stadium?

86. In which season did the Tigers first pass the 200 mark in home runs?

87. How many did they hit that year?

88. Following the 1962 season, the Tigers took off on a barnstorming tour. Where did their travels take them?

89. Who did Detroit obtain in the 1963 deal which sent Jim Bunning and Gus Triandos to the Philadelphia Phillies?

History — Questions

90. Who did the Yankees offer Detroit in exchange for Al Kaline in 1964?

91. What was unusual about Detroit's 2-1 victory over Baltimore on April 30, 1967?

92. What embarrassing injury did Al Kaline suffer in the summer of 1967?

93. Which players did the Tigers lose to the Seattle Pilots in the 1968 expansion draft?

94. Which players did the Tigers lose to the Kansas City Royals in the 1968 expansion draft?

95. Who were the players elected to the All-Time Detroit Tiger team, as selected by the fans, in 1969?

96. Denny McLain's off-the-field activities in 1969 came to a head at the All-Star break. What development caused general manager Jim Campbell to crack down on McLain's exploits?

97. What was the reason for McLain's suspension in mid-February of 1970?

98. What was Bowie Kuhn's decision on the matter following his investigation?

History — Questions

99. McLain was suspended again on August 28, 1970. What was the reason this time?

100. McLain was finally traded to Washington shortly before the start of the 1970 World Series. Who else was involved in the deal?

101. Who did Detroit honor with a "day" on August 2, 1970?

102. Which three members of the Tiger pitching staff were sidelined prior to the start of the 1971 regular season?

103. Detroit won the American League East title in 1972 by a half-game over the Boston Red Sox. How was this possible?

104. What was the nickname given to Billy Martin's veteran 1972-1973 teams?

105. Which two radio broadcasters have teamed up for Tiger games continuously since 1973—the longest such current streak in the AL?

106. On their way to a last-place finish in 1975, the Bengals set a club record for consecutive losses. How many games did they lose in a row?

History — Questions

107. Name the pitcher who ended the losing streak.

108. Which slugger did the Tigers acquire from San Diego in November of 1974?

109. Which slugger did the Tigers obtain in the Mickey Lolich deal in late 1975?

110. Which players did the Tigers lose to the Toronto Blue Jays in the 1976 expansion draft?

111. Which players did the Tigers lose to the Seattle Mariners in the 1976 expansion draft?

112. In which year was Tiger Stadium sold to the city of Detroit, then leased back to the Tigers for 30 years?

113. What was the selling price?

114. The last time Detroit had the best record of any team in spring training was in 1981. How did they do in the regular season that year?

115. Who injured his knee during a 1982 brawl with the Minnesota Twins, when he foolishly attempted a karate kick?

History — Questions

116. The Tigers began the 1984 season in incredible fashion. What was their record after 40 games?

117. What unusual incident happened to Lou Whitaker at the 1985 All-Star game?

118. Who did the Tigers send to Atlanta in exchange for Doyle Alexander in August of 1987?

119. What was unusual about the Minnesota-Detroit game of August 20, 1987?

120. Whose home run accounted for the only run in Detroit's pennant-clinching win over Toronto on the final day of the 1987 season?

121. Who hurled the shutout for the Tigers?

122. Which Tiger played every position but pitcher during the 1987 season?

Answers

1. Bennett Park (1901-1911)

2. Charlie Bennett, a former catcher for the National League Detroit Wolverines in the 1880s. He later lost both his legs in a train accident in 1894.

3. The field was laid out over a layer of cobblestones.

4. Emil Frisk

5. Trailing 13-4, in the bottom of the ninth, the Tigers exploded for ten runs to defeat the Milwaukee Brewers, 14-13.

6. First baseman Pop Dillon

7. He had four doubles in the game.

History — Answers

8. George Stallings

9. Shortstop Kid Elberfeld, at .310. Utilityman Sport McAllister also reached the magic figure, hitting .301.

10. Elmer Flick

11. Wild Bill Donovan

12. 24

13. Lil' Rastus

14. Fenway Park in Boston

15. Al Travers

16. He became a Catholic priest.

17. Detroit lost to Philadelphia, 24-2, with Travers surrendering all the runs for a dubious major league record.

18. Playing third base for the Bengals, Irvin slammed two triples in three at-bats, for a lifetime batting average of .667, and a lifetime slugging percentage of 2.000.

19. Billy Maharg

20. Outfielder Bill Leinhauser

History — Answers

21. A record 26

22. 78

23. Lu Blue (1B), Ralph Young (2B), Bob Jones (3B), Donie Bush (SS), Bobby Veach (LF), Ty Cobb (CF), Harry Heilmann (RF), and Johnny Bassler (C)

24. Ralph Young (.299) and Donie Bush (.281)

25. In sixth place, 27 games behind the Yankees

26. Screwballer Carl Hubbell

27. Johnny Neun

28. Pinky Hargrave (brother Bubbles)

29. He stroked three singles and a home run, and had a steal of home.

30. Dale Alexander

31. No. He came to the plate only 454 times, well below the 502 appearances which would be required by present rules for a 154-game schedule (3.1 appearances for each game on a team's schedule).

History — Answers

32. Catcher Johnny Pasek (and $100,000)

33. Outfielder John (Rocky) Stone

34. First baseman Jack Burns

35. A pitch from Yankee hurler Bump Hadley struck him in the head in a 1937 game, knocking him unconscious and fracturing his skull in three places.

36. Ray Hayworth

37. He was the pitcher who surrendered Ty Cobb's last big-league hit, while Cobb was with the Athletics (September 3, 1928).

38. Its name was changed to Briggs Stadium.

39. Bob Feller. He struck out 18 Bengals in Detroit's 4-1 win.

40. Harry Eisenstat

41. Moving to the Browns were Vern Kennedy, Bob Harris, George Gill, Roxie Lawson, Chet Laabs and Mark Christman. Coming over to the Tigers were Red Kress, Beau Bell, Bobo Newsom and Jim Walkup.

History — Answers

42. They defeated the Philadelphia Athletics by a score of 5-0.

43. On June 20, 1939, at Shibe Park, Philadelphia

44. New York's Atley Donald (12), and Chicago's John Rigney (11)

45. Dick Bartell. Billy Rogell went over to Chicago.

46. Floyd Giebell

47. Oscar Vitt

48. None. He ended his career with a 3-1 mark.

49. Outfielder Rip Radcliff of the Browns

50. The University of Michigan

51. The Brooklyn Dodgers

52. Evansville, Indiana

53. Al Benton, Charlie Gehringer, Johnny Lipon, Barney McCosky and Birdie Tebbetts

54. Jimmy Bloodworth, Tommy Bridges,

History — Answers

Rip Radcliff, Virgil Trucks and Hal White

55. 1944

56. Dizzy Trout (2.12) and Hal Newhouser (2.22)

57. Hal Newhouser (1.81) and Al Benton (2.02)

58. Outfielder Hoot Evers and second baseman Eddie Mayo

59. Outfielder Barney McCosky

60. They defeated the Philadelphia Athletics, 4-1.

61. June 15, 1948

62. Art Houtteman

63. All 19 runs in the game scored as a result of home runs.

64. Eleven—five by the Tigers and six by the Yankees

65. Art Houtteman and Ray Herbert

66. To help celebrate the 250th anniversary of the city's founding

History — Answers

67. At the University of Wisconsin. He never played in the minors.

68. Walt Dropo, Fred Hatfield, Johnny Pesky, Don Lenhardt, and Bill Wight, who came to Detroit; and George Kell, Johnny Lipon, Hoot Evers, and Dizzy Trout, who moved on to Boston

69. They finished in eighth place for the only time in the franchise's history.

70. Bob Miller, Al Kaline and Reno Bertoia

71. Mel Ott

72. All three headed syndicates which attempted to buy the Tigers in 1956.

73. Frank Lary (21-13) and Billy Hoeft (20-14)

74. In fifth place, 15 games behind New York

75. Detroit sent Bill Tuttle, Jim Small, Duke Maas, John Tsitouris, Frank House, Kent Hadley and Jim McManus to the Athletics in exchange for Billy Martin, Gus Zernial, Lou Skizas, Tom Morgan, Maury McDermott and Tim Thompson.

History — Answers

76. Billy Martin

77. Play-by-play announcer Mel Ott was killed in an automobile accident.

78. Don Mossi and Ray Narleski

79. Ernie Harwell

80. Pete Burnside

81. Batting champion Harvey Kuenn

82. Pitchers Aubrey Gatewood and Bob Sprout, catcher Bob Rodgers and infielders Eddie Yost and Steve Bilko

83. Pitchers Pete Burnside, Dave Sisler and infielder Coot Veal.

84. Infielder Steve Demeter

85. January 1, 1961

86. 1962

87. 209

88. Hawaii, South Korea and Japan

89. Outfielder Don Demeter and pitcher Jack Hamilton

History — Answers

90. Roger Maris

91. The Tigers won the game despite being no-hit by the duo of Steve Barber and Stu Miller.

92. A broken finger incurred when he slammed his bat into the batrack after striking out.

93. Pitcher Mike Marshall, infielder Ray Oyler and outfielder Wayne Comer

94. Pitchers Jon Warden, Bill Butler and Dick Drago

95. Hank Greenberg (1B), Charlie Gehringer (2B), George Kell (3B), Billy Rogell (SS), Ty Cobb (OF), Harry Heilmann (OF), Al Kaline (OF), Mickey Cochrane (C), Denny McLain (RHP) and Hal Newhouser (LHP)

96. McLain flew home for a dental appointment, but didn't return to Washington in time for the game—a game he was scheduled to start. McLain then left in the middle of the contest, stranding teammate Mickey Lolich and his wife, who were expecting to leave with him.

History — Answers

97. Commissioner Bowie Kuhn suspended McLain because of allegations that McLain had put up money to finance a bookmaking operation. The suspension was indefinite, while Kuhn continued his investigation into the charges.

98. Kuhn suspended McLain until July 1.

99. He was suspended by the Tigers for dousing two reporters with buckets of water. Shortly thereafter, he was suspended for the rest of the season by Commissioner Kuhn for allegedly carrying a gun.

100. In addition to McLain, the Tigers sent Norm McRae, Don Wert and Elliott Maddox to the Senators in exchange for Ed Brinkman, Joe Coleman, Jim Hannan and Aurelio Rodriguez.

101. Al Kaline

102. John Hiller, who suffered a heart attack; Les Cain, who had a sore shoulder; and Joe Coleman, who suffered a fractured skull when he was beaned by a line drive.

History — Answers

103. Due to the player strike at the beginning of the season, it was decided that any games missed would not be replayed. The Tigers thus finished with an 86-70 record, while Boston, who played one less game, finished at 85-70.

104. The Over-the-Hill Gang

105. Ernie Harwell and Paul Carey

106. Nineteen, one short of then-American League mark of 20, recorded by Boston in 1906, Philadelphia in 1916 and Philadelphia in 1943

107. Ray Bare broke the streak with a 2-0 win over the Angels.

108. Nate Colbert

109. Rusty Staub, from the New York Mets

110. Pitchers Dennis DeBarr and Dave Lemanczyk

111. Infielder-outfielder Dan Meyer and pitchers Frank MacCormack and Bill Laxton

112. 1977

113. $1

History — Answers

114. They finished with the fourth-best record in the AL East—on a cumulative basis—in the strike-shortened split season.

115. Dave Rozema

116. 35-5

117. His uniform failed to arrive, and he was forced to play the game in a souvenir uniform purchased from a stadium vendor.

118. Minor league pitcher John Smoltz

119. Until two were out in the bottom of the 8th inning, no Twin player had an assist in the contest. Johnny Grubb grounded out to short for the Tigers' final out.

120. Larry Herndon's

121. Frank Tanana

122. Mike Heath

Post-season Play

1907

1. Prior to winning their first pennant in 1907, what had been Detroit's highest finish in the American League?

2. Who was Detroit's opponent in the Series?

3. Who was the manager of the Bengals?

4. What was the result of Detroit's first-ever World Series game?

5. What unfortunate event "snatched Detroit from the jaws of victory" in that game?

6. The Cubs went on to sweep the next four games from the Tigers. How many runs did Detroit score in those contests?

Post-season Play — Questions

7. Whose shutout in the final game put the Bengals out of their misery?

8. Ty Cobb and Sam Crawford finished 1-2 in the 1907 AL batting race, hitting .350 and .323, respectively. How did they do in the Series?

9. Chicago ran wild against catchers Boss Schmidt and Fred Payne. How many stolen bases did they collect?

10. Who was the leading hitter in the Series for the Tigers?

11. What was unusual about the attendance figures for the Series?

12. What was significant about George Mullin's appearance in the Series?

13. How did he fare in the Classic?

1908

14. In the 1908 Series, the Cubs were the Tigers' opponent once again, as Chicago won their third straight pennant the day after the regular season ended. What were the circumstances surrounding their victory?

Post-season Play — Questions

15. What was Detroit's margin of victory over second-place Cleveland in the regular season?

16. In a game played in a steady rain, Detroit led Chicago, 6-5, heading into the ninth inning of Game 1. The Cubs, however, put together six consecutive hits for five runs and a 10-6 victory. Who was the victim of the late-inning attack?

17. Which Tiger garnered the first pinch-hit in a World Series?

18. Which pitcher held Chicago to one hit through seven innings of Game 2, only to lose when the Cubs rallied for six runs in the bottom of the eighth?

19. Who was the first Tiger hurler to post a victory in World Series action, defeating Chicago, 8-3, in Game 3?

20. The Tigers managed only seven hits in the final two games of the Series, losing by scores of 3-0 and 2-0. Who tossed the shutouts for the Cubs?

21. The final game of the Series holds what dubious distinction?

Post-season Play — Questions

22. Ty Cobb and Sam Crawford once again finished 1-2 in the AL batting race. How did they do in this Series?

1909

23. In 1909, Detroit edged Philadelphia by three-and-a-half games to take their third consecutive American League pennant. Who were their National League opponents?

24. The 1909 confrontation signified what World Series "first"?

25. What was unusual about the pattern of victories in the Series?

26. How did Pittsburgh baserunners perform against catchers Boss Schmidt and Oscar Stanage?

27. The big three of the Pittsburgh pitching staff were Howie Camnitz, Vic Willis and Lefty Leifield, who won 25, 22 and 19 games, respectively, during the regular season. How many wins did they account for in the Series?

28. Name the rookie hurler who won three games for the Pirates.

Post-season Play — Questions

29. For the first time in history, the batting champions of the two leagues met in the Series. How did Ty Cobb and Honus Wagner fare in their head-to-head competition?

30. For the third consecutive year, the Tigers lost the final game of the Series by means of a shutout. By what score did Babe Adams defeat them?

31. Who was the leading hitter in the Series?

32. Game 5 saw the first home runs hit by Tiger players in World Series action. Who connected for Detroit?

33. Which Detroit pitcher became the first hurler in history to lose the final game of the Series in two consecutive years?

1934

34. Who was the player-manager who led the Tigers to their first pennant in 25 years, guiding them to the top in 1934?

35. Three future Hall-of-Famers, each of whose last name began with the letter *G*, were regulars on the 1934 squad. Can you name them?

Post-season Play — Questions

36. Who evened the Series at one game apiece by hurling a 12-inning complete game victory over Bill Walker of the Cardinals in Game 2?

37. Dizzy Dean made an appearance as a pinch-runner for St. Louis in Game 4. Whose throw beaned him and knocked him out of the game?

38. When Ducky Medwick collided with Detroit third baseman Marv Owen in the sixth inning of Game 7, Tiger fans showered the field with garbage and caused Commissioner Landis to remove Medwick from the game in order to prevent a possible riot. What was the score at the time?

39. The Tigers went on to lose the game by a score of 11-0, marking the fourth consecutive time they were shut out in the final game of a Series. Who whitewashed them this time?

40. Four different Detroit pitchers were charged with the four losses. Can you identify them?

41. Which two hurlers accounted for all the St. Louis wins in the Series, taking two games apiece?

Post-season Play — Questions

42. Who led the Tigers in hitting?

43. Who became the first Tiger to have a single, double, triple and home run in the same Series?

1935

44. The Tigers won the 1935 Series over Chicago, four games to two, with Lon Warneke receiving credit for both Cub victories. Who won a pair of games for Detroit?

45. In the sixth—and final—game, the Tigers and Cubs were tied, 3-3, when Stan Hack led off the Chicago ninth with a triple. How did pitcher Bridges respond to the threat?

46. With two out and a runner on second in the bottom of the ninth, Goose Goslin singled to right field to score the winning run and give Detroit its first World Championship. Who scored the winning tally?

47. Play in the Classic was marred by a series of arguments between umpire George Moriarty and several of the Cubs. How did Commissioner Landis handle the situation?

Post-season Play — Questions

48. How did American League MVP Hank Greenberg perform in the Series?

49. Why were his contributions to the Detroit cause so limited?

50. Third baseman Marv Owen moved over to first to take Greenberg's place. Who replaced Owen at third?

51. How did Owen and Clifton do in the Series?

52. Who led Detroit in hitting?

53. Who hit the Tigers' only home run of the Series?

54. What sad note followed Detroit's Series victory?

55. Who purchased control of the Tigers following the Series?

1940

56. The Tigers qualified for the 1940 Series on the next-to-last day of the season, beating out the Indians by one game. What was significant about the .584 winning percentage compiled by Detroit?

Post-season Play — Questions

57. Who recorded two of the Tigers' three victories in the Classic?

58. What personal tragedy marred this pitcher's win in Game 1?

59. After Detroit won the opener, the Reds came back and defeated the Tigers in Game 2 to tie the Series. That game marked the end of a streak of ten consecutive victories for the American League in Series competition. Which Cincinnati pitcher broke the string?

60. After shutting out the Reds in Game 5, Newsom returned to the mound with only one day's rest, after Walters had shut out the Tigers in Game 6 to tie the Series. How did Bobo fare in the decisive contest?

61. Two Detroit players hit for a "Series cycle," each with at least one single, double, triple and home run over the course of the seven games. Name them.

62. Who led Detroit in hitting, batting at a .360 clip?

Post-season Play — Questions

63. In addition to Greenberg and Higgins, which two other Tigers homered in the Series?

64. Detroit pitchers allowed fewer runs than the Cincinnati hurlers, as the Tigers outscored the Reds, 28 to 22. Who topped the Bengals in ERA?

65. Schoolboy Rowe led AL pitchers in winning percentage during the regular season with an .842 mark, based on a 16-3 record. How did he fare against Cincinnati?

1945

66. What was sports editor Warren Brown's comment on the 1945 wartime Series between the Tigers and Cubs?

67. Hank Greenberg's grand slam against the St. Louis Browns clinched the pennant for the Tigers on the last day of the season. Who finished second to Detroit, only one-and-a-half games behind them?

68. As they had done in their last Series appearance against Chicago in 1935, the Tigers failed to score in the first game. Who blanked Detroit on six hits?

Post-season Play — Questions

69. Virgil Trucks evened the Series the next day, but the Tigers were shut out, once again, in Game 3. Who hurled the one-hit masterpiece for the Cubs?

70. Who recorded the only hit for the Tigers?

71. How many games had Trucks won for Detroit in the regular season?

72. In the Cubs' 8-7, 12-inning win in Game 6, the two teams set a Series record for most players used in one game. How many saw action?

73. Which Tiger knocked pitcher Passeau out of the box in Game 6 with a drive off his finger which ripped his nail?

74. Whose embarrassing fall between third base and home cost the Tigers a run in Game 6?

75. Name the Tiger who had an error taken away from him five hours after Game 6 ended.

76. Whose three-run double in the first inning of Game 7 gave Detroit a 5-0 lead, which paved the way for their 9-3 victory?

Post-season Play — Questions

77. Who was the pitcher of record for Chicago in each of the final three games of the Series?

78. Hal Newhouser posted two of Detroit's wins, and set a new strikeout mark for a seven-game Series in the process. How many batters did he fan?

79. Who led Detroit in batting, compiling a .379 average?

80. Five of Detroit's 12 extra-base hits were accounted for by one player. Who was he?

81. What was the Tigers' team batting average for the Series?

1968

82. Al Kaline got the chance to play in this, his first World Series, when manager Mayo Smith broke up his regular outfield to make a spot for Kaline. Who was shifted?

83. How did Ray Oyler perform in the regular season?

Post-season Play — Questions

84. For the third time in their last four Series appearances, Detroit was shut out in the opener. Who performed the trick this time?

85. What was special about the performance?

86. Mickey Lolich was the hero of the Series for the Tigers with three victories. How many games did he win during the regular season?

87. What rare event marked Lolich's 8-1 victory over Nelson Briles in Game 2?

88. When Gibson defeated the Tigers in Game 4, he set a Series record in the process. What was it?

89. A turning point in the Series came in the fifth inning of Game 5, with the Cardinals ahead, 3-2. Which St. Louis star made a mistake which cost the Birds a run, and seemed to signal a change in momentum in the game?

90. What Series record did the Tigers tie in the third inning of Game 6?

91. Whose grand slam was the big blow of the frame?

Post-season Play—Questions

92. What Series record did Dick McAuliffe tie that inning?

93. A key inning for Lolich in Game 7 was the sixth. What was unusual about the inning?

94. Whose misjudged fly ball proved to be the key play in the Tigers' three-run seventh inning in the deciding game?

95. How did Al Kaline perform in the Series?

96. Kaline did not lead the Bengals in batting average. Who did?

97. How many Tigers did Bob Gibson fan in his three complete games?

1972

98. The opening game of the ALCS against Oakland went into the 11th inning with the score tied, 1-1. Who homered for the Tigers to give them the lead?

99. The A's pulled the game out in the bottom half of the inning when two runs scored on a pinch-hit single. Who was the seldom-used lefty who got the big hit?

Post-season Play — Questions

100. Which A's hurler shut out the Bengals, 5-0, in Game 2?

101. Game 2 was marked by an ugly incident in the seventh inning. What were the circumstances?

102. Down two games to none, the Tigers bounced back, winning Game 3 by a score of 3-0, behind Joe Coleman. What ALCS record did Coleman set in the game?

103. The Game 4 rematch between Mickey Lolich and Catfish Hunter again went into extra innings tied at one apiece. The A's pushed across two runs in the top half of the inning to take the lead, but the Tigers rallied in the home half to score three runs and win the game, 4-3. Who drove in the winning tally?

104. Who were the starting pitchers in the fifth, and deciding, game of the Series?

105. What was the score of the final game?

106. Who was Detroit's leading hitter in the Series?

Post-season Play — Questions

1984

107. In the ALCS, Detroit swept Kansas City in three games to move into the World Series against San Diego. Who was the Most Valuable Player of the ALCS?

108. Which pitcher led the Bengals in ERA, strikeouts, and innings pitched in the LCS?

109. With Detroit leading 3-2, in the Series opener, the pivotal play of the game occurred, when San Diego's leadoff batter in the seventh was thrown out trying to stretch a double into a triple. Can you name the player?

110. Whose two-run double in the 11th inning was the winning blow in Game 2?

111. The key hit in Game 3 was a two-run homer in the second inning by the man in the number nine slot in the Tiger batting order. Who slugged the upper deck shot?

112. The Tigers took Game 4 by a 4-2 score. Who drove in all the Detroit runs with a pair of two-run homers?

Post-season Play — Questions

113. Detroit took a 4-3 lead in Game 5 when a runner scored from third base on a high popup caught by an infielder. Who was this fleet-footed runner?

114. What other contributions did he make in Game 5?

115. Who was voted the Most Valuable Player of the Series?

116. The 1984 Fall Classic was the Tigers' first in which they were not shut out in at least one game. How many times were they blanked in their previous 51 Series contests?

117. What "first" did Sparky Anderson accomplish by leading the Tigers to the title?

118. Despite Detroit's overall domination of the baseball scene in 1984, the Padres actually outhit them in the Series. What were the averages of the two clubs?

119. Who were the only two men in uniform for Detroit on both the 1968 and 1984 World Championship teams?

Post-season Play—Questions

1987

120. The Tigers took a 5-4 lead into the bottom half of the eighth inning in Game 1 of the ALCS, but then the roof fell in, and Minnesota scored four times for an 8-5 win. Who drove in two runs for Detroit, stroking a single and home run in the game?

121. The Tigers blew another lead in the second game, finally falling, 6-3. Who was the losing pitcher for Detroit, ending his 11-0 mastery over the Twins in Minnesota?

122. The hero of Game 3 was an outfielder who hit only six home runs all year. Whose two-run blast in the eighth inning gave the Bengals a come-from-behind, 7-6 victory?

123. Who was the only Detroit hurler to record a victory in the LCS?

124. Who had an RBI in four of the five games for the Tigers?

125. Who was the losing pitcher in both the first and last games of the LCS?

Post-season Play — Questions

126. The Tigers hit seven home runs in the five-game Series against Minnesota. Who accounted for two of the four-baggers?

Answers

1. Third, in 1901 and 1905

2. The Chicago Cubs

3. Rookie skipper Hughie Jennings

4. It ended in a 3-3 tie. The game was called on account of darkness after 12 innings.

5. Detroit catcher Charlie (Boss) Schmidt dropped a third strike which would have ended the game in the ninth inning. The tying run scored on the play, sending the contest into extra frames.

6. Only three, the same number they tallied in Game 1. The final scores were 3-1, 5-1, 6-1 and 2-0.

7. Mordecai (Three-Finger) Brown's

Post-season Play — Answers

8. Cobb batted .200, with four hits in 20 at-bats, and Crawford hit .238, on five for 21.

9. Eighteen, including six by leadoff man Jimmy Slagle

10. First baseman Claude Rossman, who hit an even .400, on eight for 20.

11. The attendance went down for each succeeding game, from 24,377 to 21,901 to 13,114 to 11,306 to 7,370.

12. He became the only pitcher to appear in a World Series after losing 20 games in the regular season.

13. He lost Games 2 and 5, though he surrendered only three earned runs in 17 innings.

14. The Cubs met the Giants in a replay of the famous "Merkle boner" game which had been contested earlier in the season. The game was to be replayed only if it would have an effect on the final standings. When the teams finished in a tie for first, the Cubs and Giants met to determine the champion. Chicago won, as Three-Finger Brown defeated Christy Mathewson, 4-2.

Post-season Play — Answers

15. One-half game. Detroit finished at 90-63, and Cleveland finished at 90-64.

16. Twenty-four-game winner Ed Summers

17. Catcher Ira Thomas, in Game 1

18. Wild Bill Donovan

19. George Mullin

20. Three-Finger Brown in Game 4, and Orval Overall in the clincher

21. It was attended by fewer fans than any game in World Series history (6,210).

22. Cobb batted a robust .368 to lead the club. Crawford repeated his performance of the year before, hitting .238.

23. The Pittsburgh Pirates

24. It was the first Series to go the full seven-game limit.

25. The clubs alternated wins, with Pittsburgh taking each of the odd-numbered games, and the Tigers taking the even ones.

26. They stole 18 bases, tying the record of the 1907 Cubs.

Post-season Play — Answers

27. None

28. Babe Adams, who was 12-3 in the regular season. Thirteen-game winner Nick Maddox won the other.

29. Wagner led Pittsburgh with a .333 average, while Triple Crown winner Cobb dropped to .231.

30. 8-0

31. Detroit second baseman Jim Delahanty, who batted .346, with nine hits in 26 at-bats.

32. Outfielders Davy Jones and Sam Crawford

33. Wild Bill Donovan (1908, 1909)

34. Mickey Cochrane

35. Charlie Gehringer, Hank Greenberg and Goose Goslin

36. Schoolboy Rowe

37. Billy Rogell's

38. St. Louis 9, Detroit 0

Post-season Play — Answers

39. Dizzy Dean

40. Game 1—General Crowder; Game 3—Tommy Bridges; Game 6—Schoolboy Rowe; and Game 7—Eldon Auker

41. Dizzy Dean and Paul (Daffy) Dean

42. Charlie Gehringer (.379, on 11-29)

43. Hank Greenberg. He had five singles, two doubles, one triple and one home run against the Cards.

44. Tommy Bridges

45. Bridges struck out shortstop Billy Jurges, retired opposing pitcher Larry French on a comebacker, and got left fielder Augie Galan to fly out, stranding Hack at third.

46. Player-manager Mickey Cochrane

47. After the Series, he fined Moriarty, Chicago manager Charlie Grimm, and Cub players Woody English, Billy Herman and Billy Jurges for using improper language.

48. He batted .167, with only one hit in six at-bats.

Post-season Play — Answers

49. He suffered a broken wrist in Game 2 and missed the rest of the Series.

50. Herman (Flea) Clifton

51. They combined for an .028 batting average, with just one hit in 36 at-bats (Owen 1-20, and Clifton 0-16).

52. Right fielder Pete Fox, who batted .385 with ten hits in 26 at-bats.

53. Hank Greenberg, in Game 2

54. Tiger President Frank Navin died of a heart attack while horseback riding on November 13, less than five weeks after the Series.

55. Walter O. Briggs, Sr.

56. It was the lowest percentage, up to that time, for an American League pennant winner.

57. Bobo Newsom

58. Newsom's father, who attended the game, died early the next morning.

59. Bucky Walters

Post-season Play — Answers

60. He allowed only seven hits and two runs, losing by a score of 2-1.

61. Hank Greenberg and Pinky Higgins

62. Right fielder Bruce Campbell

63. Bruce Campbell and Rudy York

64. Rookie Johnny Gorsica (0.79, giving up only one run in 11⅓ innings pitched)

65. He was knocked out early twice, surrendering 12 hits and seven runs in only three-and-two-thirds innings, for a 17.18 ERA. He lost Games 2 and 4.

66. "I don't think either team is capable of winning."

67. The Washington Senators

68. Hank Borowy

69. Claude Passeau

70. Rudy York

71. None. He returned to the team from military service less than a week before the Series began, and made only one appearance in the regular season, with no record.

Post-season Play — Answers

72. Thirty-eight—19 for each club

73. Third baseman Jimmy Outlaw

74. Pinch-hitter Chuck Hostetler's

75. Left fielder Hank Greenberg. A base hit which hopped over his shoulder was changed from a single and error to a double.

76. Catcher Paul Richards'

77. Hank Borowy. He started and lost Game 5, hurled four innings of relief for the victory in Game 6, and started and lost Game 7.

78. Twenty-two, in 20⅔ innings.

79. Center fielder Roger (Doc) Cramer

80. Hank Greenberg, who had three doubles and both of the Tigers' home runs.

81. Only .223, 40 points below the mark recorded by the losing Cubs.

82. Center fielder Mickey Stanley moved to shortstop, replacing Ray Oyler, right fielder Jim Northrup shifted to center and Kaline was inserted in right.

Post-season Play — Answers

83. He batted only .135 as one of the two shortstop "regulars." The other, Tom Matchick, batted .203.

84. Bob Gibson

85. Gibson fanned 17 in the game for a Series record.

86. 17

87. Lolich hit the only home run of his professional career.

88. The win marked Gibson's seventh consecutive complete-game victory in Series competition.

89. Lou Brock. Brock was thrown out at home when he failed to slide while attempting to score on a base hit by Julian Javier. Detroit came back to win the contest.

90. They scored ten runs to tie the standard set by the 1929 Philadelphia Athletics for most runs in a single inning.

91. Jim Northrup

92. He became the second player in history to walk twice in one inning.

Post-season Play — Answers

93. Lolich picked two batters off base in the inning (Lou Brock and Curt Flood)

94. Jim Northrup's. After breaking in and slipping, center fielder Curt Flood could not catch up with Northrup's drive, which went for a two-out, two-run triple.

95. He batted .379 on 11 hits in 29 times up. He stroked two doubles and two homers, and drove in eight runs.

96. Norm Cash, at .385

97. Thirty-five—a new record for a single Series.

98. Al Kaline

99. Gonzalo Marquez

100. John (Blue Moon) Odom

101. After being struck on the foot by a pitch from Detroit's Lerrin LaGrow, the A's Bert "Campy" Campaneris threw his bat at the hurler. Both players were ejected, with Campaneris fined and suspended for the rest of the LCS.

102. He fanned a record 14 batters.

Post-season Play — Answers

103. Jim Northrup

104. Woody Fryman for the Tigers and Blue Moon Odom for the A's.

105. The A's edged Detroit, 2-1.

106. Jim Northrup (.357, on five for 14)

107. Kirk Gibson, who batted .417 (five for 12), with a double, home run, and two RBIs

108. Milt Wilcox, with a 0.00 ERA, 8 strikeouts and 8 innings pitched

109. Designated hitter Kurt Bevacqua

110. Johnny Grubb's

111. Third baseman Marty Castillo

112. Alan Trammell

113. Kirk Gibson

114. He hit two home runs and drove in five runs.

115. Alan Trammell, who batted .450 (nine for 20), with a double, two homers and six runs batted in

Post-season Play — Answers

116. Ten times

117. He became the first manager in history to win a Series title in both leagues.

118. Detroit .253; San Diego .265

119. Dick Tracewski and Gates Brown. Both were players in 1968 and coaches in 1984.

120. Catcher Mike Heath

121. Jack Morris

122. Pat Sheridan

123. Reliever Jim Henneman

124. Kirk Gibson

125. Doyle Alexander

126. Outfielder Chet Lemon

At the Plate and on the Bases

1. What was sportswriter Ring Lardner's advice on how to retire Ty Cobb?

2. Which Detroit rookie led the American League in hits in 1929, with 215?

3. Although he finished his nine-year career with a .304 batting mark, this catcher of the 1920s hit only one home run in 2,319 at-bats. Can you identify him?

4. Who was the last Tiger to lead the AL in runs batted in?

5. Which Detroit players have hit a home run in their first big league at-bat?

6. Which of these were hit as pinch-hitters?

At the Plate and on the Bases—Questions

7. Which hitter once said, "Every great batter works on the theory that the pitcher is more afraid of him than he is of the pitcher"?

8. Which player hit Detroit's first two home runs of the 1982 season, but no others the rest of the year?

9. Name the Tiger batting champion who was drafted by the Chicago Bears of the NFL.

10. After batting .240 as a rookie in 1905, Ty Cobb never again hit below .300. How many seasons in a row did he surpass the magic mark?

11. How many times in his career did Sam Crawford reach double figures for triples in a season?

12. How old was Charlie Gehringer when he won his first, and only, batting title?

13. Which Tiger shortstop had a record seven consecutive hits in a 12-inning contest in 1970?

14. What was unusual about Harry Heilmann's four American League batting championships?

At the Plate and on the Bases — Questions

15. What was his batting average over that span?

16. Which quiet man was Ty Cobb speaking of when he said, "He'd say hello at the start of spring training and goodbye at the end of the season, and the rest of the time he let his bat and glove do all the talking for him"?

17. Which Detroit outfielder hit four home runs in four consecutive at-bats in 1982?

18. In 15 seasons, this pitcher batted 531 times, slugging just three home runs. All three came in 1957, including two on the same day. Who was this left-hander?

19. Name the Detroit outfielder who stroked 201 hits and a league-leading 45 doubles as a rookie in 1929.

20. Which slugger once said, "I owe my success to expansion pitching, a short right field fence, and my hollow bats"?

21. Which Tiger star collected over 3,000 hits in his career, yet finished with a batting average below .300?

At the Plate and on the Bases—Questions

22. The last two Tigers to hit for the cycle both did so in 1950. Name them.

23. Which Tiger is the only player in history to lead both the American League and National League in homers?

24. What was Ty Cobb's lifetime batting average with Detroit?

25. Which former Giant first baseman led the 1958 Bengals in home runs with 20?

26. Who won the last Tiger "Triple Crown," leading the team in batting average, home runs and RBIs?

27. Ty Cobb owns the two longest batting streaks in Detroit history (40 games and 35 games). Who is the only other Tiger to hit in over 30 consecutive games?

28. Who was the first Tiger to reach double figures in doubles, triples, home runs and stolen bases in a single season?

29. Which Tiger reached double figures in homers for a season, yet had fewer strikeouts than four-baggers?

At the Plate and on the Bases — Questions

30. Name the Detroit catcher whose record included years of batting .346 and .323 for the Bengals.

31. Who is the only Tiger to play all 162 games in a season without stealing a base?

32. In compiling a 4-3 mark with a 4.15 ERA as a Tiger rookie in 1955, Werner Birrer had one memorable relief stint. What did he do in that game to give rise to his nickname of "Babe"?

33. Both Lou Whitaker and Alan Trammell have each hit more than 20 homers in a season for Detroit. What were their best home run totals in the minors, for a minimum of 100 games?

34. Who were the two youngest batting champions in history?

35. Where did Al Kaline get his 3,000th big-league hit?

36. Detroit batters have won 22 American League batting titles. Of these, only three were with marks below .350. Name the players who recorded these averages.

At the Plate and on the Bases — Questions

37. Two Tigers have won AL home run titles with single-figure totals. Who were they?

38. Who held the Detroit season stolen bases record prior to Ty Cobb?

39. Which Tiger hit exactly 200 home runs in his 15 years in a Detroit uniform?

40. Ty Cobb leads all Tiger players in lifetime stolen bases with 865. Who is in second place, with exactly 400?

41. Hank Greenberg's 57th and 58th home runs of the 1938 season came in a game against St. Louis on September 27th. Who was the pitcher for the Browns?

42. Greenberg's final game before entering military service was against the Yankees on May 6, 1941. How did he perform that day?

43. How did he fare in his first game back, over four years later?

44. Which Tiger pitcher had a 5-for-5 day at the plate on August 14, 1935?

45. What was George Kell's winning margin over Ted Williams for the 1949 batting crown?

At the Plate and on the Bases — Questions

46. Which newcomer led the Tigers in steals in 1972?

47. Who once said, "Charlie Gehringer is in a rut. He hits .350 on opening day and stays there all season"?

48. Which Detroit outfielder ended his Hall of Fame career with 399 home runs?

49. Which rookie clouted 17 homers in 1976, the most by a Detroit freshman since Rudy York's 35 in 1937?

50. Can you name the Tiger first baseman who stole five bases in a game against the Yankees in 1927, then later went on to manage the New Yorkers?

51. The Tigers have had three left-handed hitting home run champions. Can you name them?

52. Al Kaline is the only player in history to hit at least 300 home runs yet never reach 30 in a season. What was his high?

53. Prior to Hank Greenberg, which other first baseman held the Bengals' single-season home run mark?

At the Plate and on the Bases — Questions

54. Who is the only player to garner over 1,000 extra-base hits in his Tiger career?

55. The only pitcher ever to stroke four hits in an Opening Day game was a Detroit hurler. Name him.

56. Who is the only AL player to ever have 100 or more RBIs at the All-Star break?

57. Which Tiger hit the last home run at the "old" Yankee Stadium?

58. Aside from Babe Ruth, no player has led the AL in slugging percentage for more successive seasons than Ty Cobb. How many years did he top the Junior Circuit?

59. When Barney McCosky stroked 200 hits in 1940 to tie for the AL lead, he tied with two future Detroit outfielders. Can you name them?

60. Which Tiger shortstop fanned only 13 times in 155 games (656 at-bats) in 1954?

61. This Tiger pitcher hit two home runs in his big-league career, which covered 138 games. Oddly enough, both came

At the Plate and on the Bases — Questions

in the same contest. Can you name this hurler?

62. What was significant about this feat?

63. What was his nickname?

64. Who is the only Tiger to hit a total of five home runs in two consecutive games?

Answers

1. "That's easy. You just take a gun and shoot him."

2. Dale Alexander

3. Johnny Bassler

4. Ray Boone. He drove in 116 runs in 1955 to tie Boston's Jackie Jensen for the top spot.

5. Hack Miller (1944), George Vico (1948), Gates Brown (1963), Bill Roman (1964), Gene Lamont (1970) and Reggie Sanders (1974)

6. Brown's and Sanders's

7. Ty Cobb

8. Enos Cabell

At the Plate and on the Bases — Answers

9. Norm Cash (1955)

10. 23

11. Seventeen consecutive years, from 1900 through 1916

12. Thirty-four. He is the oldest player this century to win a first batting crown.

13. Cesar Gutierrez (June 21)

14. They came in four consecutive odd-numbered years (1921, 1923, 1925 and 1927).

15. .380 (1,417 hits in 3,731 at-bats)

16. Charlie Gehringer

17. Larry Herndon

18. Billy Hoeft

19. Roy Johnson

20. Norm Cash

21. Al Kaline (.297, with 3,007 hits)

22. George Kell (June 2), and Hoot Evers (September 7)

At the Plate and on the Bases — Answers

23. Sam Crawford. He led the NL while with Cincinnati in 1901, and the AL with Detroit in 1908.

24. .369

25. Gail Harris

26. Steve Kemp (1979)

27. John (Rocky) Stone (34 in 1930)

28. Bobby Veach in 1920 (39, 15, 11, and 11, respectively)

29. Charlie Gehringer, twice. In 1935 he had 19 homers and 16 strikeouts, and the next year 15 homers and 13 strikeouts.

30. Johnny Bassler

31. Ed Brinkman (1966)

32. He batted two times, and slammed two three-run homers.

33. Three each

34. Al Kaline and Ty Cobb, both at age 20. Since Kaline's birthday was on December 19th, and Cobb's on

At the Plate and on the Bases — Answers

December 18th, Kaline was one day younger.

35. In his hometown of Baltimore

36. Ty Cobb (.324 in 1908), George Kell (.343 in 1949) and Al Kaline (.340 in 1955)

37. Sam Crawford (seven in 1908) and Ty Cobb (nine in 1909)

38. Ducky Holmes, with 35 in 1901. Cobb stole 49 six years later to eclipse the mark.

39. Catcher Bill Freehan

40. Donie Bush

41. Bill Cox

42. He homered his first two times up against Tiny Bonham.

43. He hit a home run which helped put the Tigers into first place (July 1, 1945).

44. Schoolboy Rowe

45. .00016. Kell batted .34291 to Williams's .34275.

At the Plate and on the Bases — Answers

46. Second baseman Tony Taylor—with five!

47. Yankee pitcher Lefty Gomez

48. Al Kaline

49. Jason Thompson

50. Johnny Neun

51. Sam Crawford (1908), Ty Cobb (1909) and Darrell Evans (1985)

52. Twenty-nine, in 1962 and 1966

53. Dale Alexander, with 25 in his rookie year of 1929. Greenberg swatted 26 in 1934, 36 in 1935, 40 in 1937, and 58 in 1938.

54. Ty Cobb (1,063)

55. Harry Coveleski (April 12, 1916)

56. Hank Greenberg, with 100 in 1935. Greenberg, who finished the year with 170, was not on the All-Star roster that year.

57. Duke Sims (1973)

At the Plate and on the Bases — Answers

58. Eight times, including six in succession, from 1907 to 1912

59. Rip Radcliff and Doc Cramer

60. Harvey Kuenn

61. Ed Summers

62. It marked the first time in modern history that a pitcher hit two homers in a game.

63. Kickapoo

64. Ty Cobb, who hit three on May 5 and two on May 6, 1925

The Brain Trust

1. How did Sparky Anderson fare in his only big-league season as a player?

2. What was the nickname of former Tiger player and manager Hughie Jennings?

3. Which former Tiger manager once said, "Open up a ballplayer's head and you know what you'd find? A lot of little broads and a jazz band"?

4. Sparky Anderson is the only manager to have won 700 or more games for two major league teams. Who is the only other pilot to have won as many as 600 games with two different clubs?

5. Which Tiger owner summed up his philosophy by stating, "I've not served as owner of this great franchise—only as its guardian"?

The Brain Trust — Questions

6. Which member of the Detroit front office was center fielder on the 1955 All-American team?

7. Can you name the five former Detroit managers who have been elected to the Hall of Fame?

8. Whom did Sparky Anderson replace as manager of the Bengals?

9. Who ran the Tigers on the field in 1936 while manager Mickey Cochrane was recovering from a nervous breakdown?

10. What was Mickey Cochrane's "3M" formula?

11. Which former Detroit manager once said, "When I get through managing, I'm going to open up a kindergarten"?

12. Which former Yankee All-Star managed the Tigers from 1949 to 1952?

13. Which former Tiger great joined the Detroit front office in 1951 as vice president and general manager?

14. Name the former Detroit manager who once hit four home runs in a game.

The Brain Trust — Questions

15. In 1954, Washington finished in sixth place, two games behind Detroit. When the Senators' manager was fired after the season, he was signed by Detroit to replace Fred Hutchinson, who had resigned. Can you name him?

16. Which former major league star replaced John McHale as general manager of Detroit in 1959?

17. How did the Tigers fare in Jimmie Dykes's managerial debut, in 1959?

18. What were the given first names of Tiger managers Bucky Harris, Red Rolfe, Mayo Smith and Sparky Anderson?

19. Which former Tiger manager was a quarterback for the Chicago Staleys of the NFL back in the 1920s?

20. While working as a broadcaster, this Tiger owner interviewed Tito of Yugoslavia, deGaulle of France, the Shah of Iran and Konrad Adenauer of Germany, among others. Name him.

21. Which Tiger manager married the daughter of a United States Senator?

The Brain Trust — Questions

22. This former Tiger pilot also scouted for Detroit. Name the man who signed Harvey Kuenn, Billy Hoeft, and Bill Tuttle, among others.

23. Which Detroit manager had three brothers who played in the major leagues?

24. Name the Detroit manager who later became a vice president of the New York Mets.

25. Which former pitcher committed suicide after being named manager of the Tigers?

26. Which four Tiger managers have won pennants while leading clubs in the National League?

27. This Tiger field manager was also an umpire, writer, vaudeville performer and inventor of improvements for the typewriter. Can you name him?

28. What historic deal did General Manager Bill DeWitt complete in early August of 1960?

29. Which Tiger coach was "traded" to the Indians in 1960?

The Brain Trust — Questions

30. Which two interim managers have piloted the Tigers to perfect records?

31. In an effort to break a losing streak in 1972, what unorthodox method did Billy Martin use in deciding upon a lineup?

32. In 1966, for the first time in history, a team lost two managers through illness in the same season. Who were these Tiger pilots?

33. Who finally finished out the year at the team's helm?

34. Which Tiger owner was raised in an orphanage and in foster homes, and entered a seminary before graduating from high school?

35. Prior to obtaining Mickey Cochrane from Philadelphia, to whom did Detroit owner Frank Navin offer the job as manager of the Tigers?

36. Which former Detroit manager died on his 81st birthday?

37. Which Tiger manager was a major in the army, and was awarded a Silver Star, a Bronze Star and a Purple Heart?

The Brain Trust — Questions

38. Who held the title of Tiger club president for a longer period of time than any other man?

39. Which Hall of Fame catcher was a coach with Detroit in 1930 and 1931?

40. Which Detroit president got his start in baseball when he was recommended to Branch Rickey as an office boy for the St. Louis Browns?

41. Name the front office man who summarized the Tigers' economic philosophy thusly: "We are constitutionally opposed to the creation of young sport millionaires."

42. To whom did John Fetzer offer the Detroit managerial job following the 1960 season?

43. Why was the offer refused?

44. When Bob Scheffing was relieved of his managerial duties in June of 1963, his entire coaching staff was also dropped—the first time in history that an entire such group was canned in mid-season. Can you name Scheffing's three coaches?

The Brain Trust — Questions

45. Who was the pitching coach fired in 1969, following an on-going dispute with manager Mayo Smith?

46. What was Billy Martin's reaction, in 1973, when he believed Cleveland hurler Gaylord Perry was throwing spitballs in a game against Detroit?

47. What was American League President Joe Cronin's reaction to the matter?

48. How did Tiger general manager Jim Campbell respond to the situation?

Answers

1. He batted .218 for Philadelphia in 1959 as the Phillies' regular second baseman.

2. Ee-Yah

3. Mayo Smith

4. Leo Durocher, with 740 for the Dodgers and 637 with the Giants (he also had 535 for the Cubs and 98 with Houston.)

5. John Fetzer

6. Vice President and General Manager Bill Lajoie, at Western Michigan University

7. Ed Barrow, Ty Cobb, Mickey Cochrane, Bucky Harris and Hughie Jennings

The Brain Trust — Answers

8. Les Moss

9. Coach Del Baker

10. "*M*agic *M*anagerial *M*aneuverings"

11. Billy Martin

12. Former third baseman Red Rolfe

13. Charlie Gehringer

14. Bobby Lowe

15. Bucky Harris

16. Rick Ferrell

17. Spearheaded by Charlie Maxwell, who slugged four home runs, they swept a doubleheader from the Yankees.

18. Stanley Harris, Robert Rolfe, Edward Smith and George Anderson

19. Chuck Dressen

20. John Fetzer

21. Bucky Harris

22. George Moriarty

The Brain Trust — Answers

23. Steve O'Neill (brothers Jim, Jack and Mike)

24. Bob Scheffing

25. Win Mercer (1903)

26. Sparky Anderson, Chuck Dressen, Fred Hutchinson and George Stallings

27. George Moriarty

28. He traded manager Jimmie Dykes to the Cleveland Indians in exchange for Tribe manager Joe Gordon.

29. Luke Appling. He went to Cleveland in exchange for Indian coach Jo-Jo White shortly after the Dykes-Gordon managerial switch.

30. Billy Hitchcock (1-0 in 1960) and Dick Tracewski (2-0 in 1979)

31. He picked names out of a hat to determine the batting order. The Tigers won the game, 3-2.

32. Chuck Dressen and Bob Swift

33. Third base coach Frank Skaff

34. Tom Monaghan

The Brain Trust — Answers

35. Babe Ruth. Navin arranged to buy Cochrane when he decided he couldn't wait for Ruth's answer.

36. Bucky Harris

37. Ralph Houk

38. Frank J. Navin (28 years, from 1908 to 1935)

39. Roger Bresnahan

40. Bill DeWitt

41. Tiger owner John Fetzer

42. Casey Stengel, who had been released by the Yankees

43. After having a medical exam, Stengel was told by his doctor that it would not be in his best interest to accept the job at that time.

44. Phil Cavarretta, George Myatt and Tom Ferrick

45. Johnny Sain

46. He ordered pitchers Joe Coleman and Fred Scherman to throw spitballs at the Indians.

The Brain Trust — Answers

47. He suspended Martin for three days.

48. He fired Martin and hired coach Joe Schultz to replace him.

The Battery

1. Which Detroit pitcher surrendered Babe Ruth's 700th home run?

2. Which Tiger won his major league debut in a game in which the opposing pitcher was his brother?

3. In 1902 the American League ERA leader posted a losing record. Who was this Detroit hurler?

4. This hurler pitched a record 23 seasons in the Pacific Coast League. Name this righthander who won 19 games as a Tiger rookie in 1922.

5. What was catcher Frank House's nickname?

6. Who is the former Tiger catcher who gained a measure of fame as Bruce

The Battery—Questions

Sutter's "personal" tutor while both were with the St. Louis Cardinals?

7. In his six-year big-league career, this tall righty finished with 35 wins, 35 losses and 35 saves. Can you name him?

8. Although he compiled only a 5-19 mark in 1952, this hurler's wins were memorable. Included among them were two no-hitters, a one-hitter and a two-hitter. Name him.

9. Who were the victims of the two no-hitters?

10. Compiling a 4-1 record in his only big-league season (1968), this lefty had even better luck in 1977 when he won $63,000 in the Ohio State Lottery. Who is he?

11. Name the wild righthander who walked 39 batters in 35⅔ innings with Detroit, and 237 batters in 213⅔ innings in his big-league career.

12. Who pitched the most years in a Tiger uniform?

13. This former Tiger catcher pitched

The Battery — Questions

ambidextrously in the minors. Who was he?

14. When this pitcher came to Detroit in 1938, he won his first nine decisions, before ending the year with a 12-9 mark. Can you name him?

15. Who was the young righthanded reliever whose 27 saves and six wins were one of the few bright spots for the Bengals' pitching staff in 1970?

16. Mickey Lolich became the workhorse of the 1971 staff. How many innings did he pitch that year?

17. Which Tiger relief pitcher was a vendor at Shea Stadium as a youngster?

18. After finishing 19-9 his rookie year of 1976, what record did Mark Fidrych compile the next season?

19. What injuries caused "The Bird" to miss most of the 1977 season?

20. Who was heralded that same year as "the new Bird"?

The Battery—Questions

21. Which two former Cincinnati hurlers combined to win 28 games for the 1978 Tigers?

22. Which Detroit reliever was nicknamed "Hot Sauce" because of his actions on the field?

23. Which Bengal pitcher made only two appearances in the 1941 season, both as pinch-hitter?

24. In 1972 this hurler appeared in games for Detroit, Oakland, San Diego and Cleveland. Can you name him?

25. Which Tiger hurler led the majors in victories during the decade of the 1940s?

26. How many games did he win over that period of time?

27. Two rookies reached double figures in wins for the 1937 team. Name them.

28. Who was the catcher who failed to tag Bob Lemon of the Indians at home plate in a crucial game in 1950?

29. What did the play become known as?

The Battery — Questions

30. Name the Tiger righthander who began the 1951 season with Detroit, was traded to the White Sox in May and went on to take the American League ERA title.

31. Which Detroit relief pitcher surrendered Frank Robinson's 500th home run?

32. This son of a Hall-of-Famer pitched for Detroit in 1959 and 1960, compiling a record of 8-8, all in relief. Can you name him?

33. Who was the rookie pitcher manager Mickey Cochrane credited with helping the Tigers get going after a slow start in their pennant-winning season of 1935?

34. Can you name the Detroit catchers of 1905 and 1963-65 who had the same name?

35. Which Tiger hurler tied for the AL lead in shutouts in 1943, then won the honor outright the next season?

36. This pitcher won his first nine decisions as a Tiger in 1929 after coming over from Cleveland. He went

The Battery — Questions

on to win exactly 200 games in his big-league career. Who was he?

37. In 1937 the Detroit pitching staff was led by Roxie Lawson, who compiled a mark of 18-7. What was unusual about his record that year?

38. What was the Cherokee Indian relief pitcher Chief Hogsett's full name?

39. Name the Detroit lefty who surrendered Harmon Killebrew's first major league homer.

40. What was noteworthy about George Mullin's no-hitter against St. Louis in 1912?

41. Which Tiger pitcher struck out 418 batters for Andalusia of the Alabama-Florida League in 1938?

42. In how many consecutive seasons did Hooks Dauss win ten or more games for the Tigers?

43. What was noteworthy about Jack Morris's 1984 no-hitter against the White Sox?

The Battery — Questions

44. Which former Tiger hurler made 874 mound appearances in his career, all but two of them in relief roles?

45. The only pitcher ever to win a World Series game on his birthday, this lefty spent parts of two seasons with Detroit toward the end of his career (1966-1967). Can you name him?

46. This righty came up to Detroit in 1960 as a starting pitcher. Of his 170 appearances with the Tigers, 101 were starts. After leaving Detroit, he made 381 further big-league appearances, all but four in relief. Who was he?

47. What was his nickname?

48. Who was the hurler who won 19 games for the Tigers in 1964, missing a chance for 20 when he was ejected from the game in his final start of the year?

49. Who were the two "Senors" in the Tiger bullpen in 1984?

50. Can you name the 17-year-old starter for the 1910 Tigers who surrendered eight runs in his only big-league appearance, yet won the game?

The Battery — Questions

51. Which four Tiger pitchers have each tossed three consecutive shutouts in a season?

52. When Willie Hernandez won the AL Cy Young award for 1984, how many save situations was he successful in?

53. Which two Detroit hurlers have won two complete game victories in a single day?

54. Only one Detroit pitcher surrendered more than one home run to Roger Maris when he slugged 61 in 1961. Who was this veteran righthander, and how many did he give up to Maris?

55. Likewise, one veteran righthander surrendered three of Babe Ruth's 60 home runs in 1927. Can you name him?

56. This Tiger hurler moved on to Houston, where he surrendered the first home run ever hit in the Astrodome (1965). Name him.

57. On what date in 1968 did Denny McLain win his 30th game?

58. Which team did he defeat for number 30?

The Battery — Questions

59. What was McLain's final record in 1970?

60. Who was the pitcher who faced midget Eddie Gaedel in a game against the Browns in 1951?

61. How did catcher Bob Swift advise his pitcher to work Gaedel?

62. Which hurler once said, "All that running and exercise can do for you is make you healthy"?

63. In 1962, this Detroit hurler led the American League in ERA with a 2.21 mark. He was not as successful as a batter, however, getting only two hits in 75 at-bats for an average of .027. Name him.

64. Which Tiger pitcher of the 1930s shared Christy Mathewson's nickname of "Big Six"?

65. Although this pitcher led AL relievers in saves in 1940, he also lost more games in relief than any other hurler. Can you name him?

66. Which Detroit righthander was one of the spitballers allowed to continue using the pitch, following the 1920 ban on freak offerings?

The Battery — Questions

67. Although he won just one game for Detroit in 1926, and eight in his entire big-league career, this righty collected 314 victories in the minors. Can you name him?

68. Which pitcher is best remembered as being the only hurler to face both Babe Ruth and Mickey Mantle in the majors?

69. Which Tiger hurler missed a perfect game in 1932 when he gave up a single to Washington's Dave Harris after retiring 26 batters in a row?

70. Who duplicated the feat in 1983 against Chicago, surrendering a base hit to Jerry Hairston after setting down the first 26 batters in the game?

71. Which team defeated Schoolboy Rowe in 1934, ending his record-tying string of 16 consecutive victories?

72. This Tiger led the Detroit staff with a 23-13 mark his rookie year of 1901. Can you name this hurler, who was only 16-33 the remainder of his career?

73. As of 1988, of the 21 men associated with the Tigers in some capacity who

The Battery — Questions

have made the Hall of Fame, only one pitched for them. Who was he?

74. What was Schoolboy Rowe's given name?

75. Which Tiger rookie struck out 19 batters and allowed 17 home runs in 94⅓ innings his maiden season of 1982?

76. What name does reliever Mike Henneman give to his rising split-fingered pitch?

77. This former Detroit reliever of the early 1960s began his career with ten consecutive losing seasons before posting a 10-7 record with Washington in 1964. Can you name him?

78. Which Tiger reliever was born in Holland?

79. Name the catching prospect who the Tigers signed to a $45,000 bonus contract in 1948.

80. Whose two-hit shutout ended the New York Yankees' 19-game winning streak in July of 1947?

The Battery — Questions

81. Cleveland hurler Johnny Allen had a 15-0 mark going into the final game of the 1937 season. Can you name the Tigers' rookie southpaw who hurled a two-hit shutout, handing Allen his only defeat of the year?

82. What was Boots Poffenberger's given name?

83. Which veteran pitcher retired mid-way through the 1936 season, after having posted a 16-10 mark the previous year?

84. Which Detroit pitcher tossed a no-hitter in both the American League and National League, and also led each circuit in strikeouts?

85. Tiger hurler Bob Cain defeated the Indians, and Bob Feller, on a one-hit, 1-0 shutout in 1952. What was unusual about the game?

86. Name the only father-son combination to pitch for the Tigers.

87. Which righthander won 221 games in his 15-year career—all with Detroit—yet never led the league in any category?

The Battery — Questions

88. Which former Tiger hurler started the first night game in World Series history, in 1971, while with the Baltimore Orioles?

89. Name the Tiger pitcher who surrendered Roger Maris's first home run in his record-setting 1961 season.

90. Which Detroit hurler was the victim of two no-hitters in 1973?

91. Although this rookie had a perfect 3-0 mark in 1948, he was traded after the season. He went on to record 208 more big-league wins. Name him.

92. Who did the Tigers obtain in the trade?

93. Hank Aaron made his final major league appearance on October 3, 1976, in a game against Detroit. Who was the last pitcher to face him, and how did Aaron do in his final at-bat?

94. Frank Lary had a 7-1 mark against the Yankees in 1958. How did he fare against the rest of the league?

95. What was Lary's lifetime record against the Yankees?

The Battery — Questions

96. What was Lary's combined record against all other teams?

97. After notching 123 wins in his ten-year career with Detroit, Lary was traded to the National League in May of 1964. Who obtained his services?

98. Who took Lary's place on the Tiger roster?

99. Who pitched the game which clinched the 1968 pennant for Detroit?

100. Which Tiger hurler is thought to have been the last man alive to have been a teammate of both Ty Cobb and Babe Ruth?

101. Which Detroit pitcher surrendered the 14th-inning home run to Red Schoendienst, which gave the National League a 4-3 victory in the 1950 All-Star game?

102. How did Steve Gromek do in his first start for the Tigers, after coming over from Cleveland in 1953?

103. Name the Tiger who once caught a game in which his brother was the umpire behind the plate.

The Battery — Questions

104. Which Detroit reliever bounced back from a heart attack, winning Comeback Player of the Year honors in 1973?

105. What were his stats that year?

106. Which Detroit star tossed a no-hitter in his first pro game?

107. How many appearances on the mound did Ty Cobb make in his Tiger career?

108. Which Tiger pitcher of the 1940s was Hall-of-Famer Bob Feller's cousin?

109. Two pitchers with the same name hurled for the Tigers, one in the 1950s, and one in 1973. Can you name them?

110. This rookie hurler had a 1-0 mark in five appearances with Detroit in 1911. He later went on to make history in Game 5 of the 1920 World Series while with Brooklyn. Who was he, and what did he do?

111. Which Tiger pitcher of the late 1950s was known as "Plowboy"?

112. Prior to Jack Morris, who had been the last Tiger hurler to win 20 games in a season?

The Battery — Questions

113. How did Denny McLain do in his major league debut?

114. How many other homers did McLain hit in his ten-year career?

Answers

1. Tommy Bridges (July 13, 1934)

2. Pat Underwood (brother Tom lost the game for Toronto, May 31, 1979)

3. Ed Siever

4. Herman Pillette

5. "Pig"

6. Mike Roarke

7. Tom Timmerman

8. Virgil Trucks

9. The Washington Senators on May 15, and the New York Yankees on August 25

10. Jon Warden

The Battery — Answers

11. Dick Weik

12. Tommy Bridges (16)

13. Paul Richards

14. Vern Kennedy

15. Tom Timmerman

16. 376

17. Ed Glynn

18. 6-4 in only 11 appearances

19. Fidrych first tore a cartilage in his right knee, then developed tendonitis in his right arm.

20. Dave Rozema, who notched 15 wins

21. Jack Billingham (15-8), and Milt Wilcox (13-12)

22. Kevin Saucier

23. Fred Hutchinson

24. Mike Kilkenny

25. Hal Newhouser

The Battery — Answers

26. One-hundred-seventy. Bob Feller was second with 137.

27. George Gill (11-4) and Boots Poffenberger (10-5)

28. Aaron Robinson. Robinson thought there was a force at the plate, when in actuality he needed to tag Lemon for the out. The run gave the Indians the game.

29. "Robinson's Rock"

30. Saul Rogovin

31. Fred Scherman (September 13, 1971)

32. Dave Sisler (son of George)

33. "Little Joe" Sullivan

34. John Eugene Sullivan and John Peter Sullivan

35. Dizzy Trout

36. George Uhle

37. He compiled the mark despite posting an ERA of 5.26.

The Battery — Answers

38. Elon Chester Hogsett

39. Billy Hoeft (1955)

40. It occurred on July 4, his 32nd birthday.

41. Virgil Trucks

42. A Detroit record 14 straight seasons (1913-1926)

43. It was the earliest date (April 7) on which a no-hitter had ever been thrown.

44. Don McMahon

45. Johnny Podres

46. Phil Regan

47. "The Vulture"

48. Dave Wickersham

49. "Senor Smoke" and "Senor Save" — Aurelio Lopez and Willie Hernandez, respectively

50. Dave Skeels

The Battery—Answers

51. Harry Coveleski (1914), Ed Wells (1926), Mickey Lolich (1964 and 1967) and Jack Morris (1986).

52. Thirty-two of 33.

53. George Mullin (September 22, 1906), and Ed Summers (September 25, 1908)

54. Frank Lary, three (numbers 31, 52 and 57).

55. Ken Holloway (numbers 28, 29 and 56)

56. Bob Bruce

57. September 14

58. The Oakland A's, by a score of 5-4

59. He was 3-5, after posting marks of 31-6 and 24-9 the previous two seasons.

60. Bob Cain

61. "Pitch him low."

62. Denny McLain

63. Hank Aguirre

The Battery — Answers

64. Eldon Auker

65. Al Benton

66. Yancy (Doc) Ayers

67. Clyde Barfoot

68. Al Benton

69. Tommy Bridges (August 5)

70. Milt Wilcox (April 15)

71. The Philadelphia Athletics (13-5, on August 29)

72. Roscoe Miller

73. Waite Hoyt (1930-1931)

74. Lynwood

75. Larry Pashnick

76. A "spoonball," as opposed to a forkball, which sinks

77. Ron Kline

78. George Zuverink (Holland, Michigan)

79. Frank House

The Battery — Answers

80. Fred Hutchinson

81. "Whistlin' Jake" Wade

82. Cletus

83. Alvin (General) Crowder

84. Jim Bunning

85. Feller also threw a one-hitter.

86. Joe Coleman, Sr. (1955) and Joe Coleman, Jr. (1971-1976)

87. Hooks Dauss

88. Pat Dobson

89. Paul Foytack

90. Jim Perry (Steve Busby's on April 27, and Nolan Ryan's on July 15)

91. Billy Pierce

92. Catcher Aaron Robinson

93. Dave Roberts. Aaron singled in the sixth inning.

94. Lary was 9-14 against the rest of the American League, for a 16-15 mark overall.

The Battery — Answers

95. 28-13

96. 100-103

97. The New York Mets

98. Denny McLain

99. Joe Sparma

100. Ed Wells

101. Ted Gray

102. He surrendered nine runs in the first inning to the Red Sox, who went on to score a modern major league record 17 runs in the frame (June 18).

103. Tom Haller (brother Bill), in 1972

104. John Hiller

105. He had a 10-5 mark and a 1.44 ERA, with a league-high 38 saves and 65 appearances.

106. Denny McLain. He hurled his gem for Harlan, Kentucky of the Appalachian League in 1962.

The Battery — Answers

107. Three—two in 1918, and one in 1925. He had no decisions, with a 3.60 ERA for five innings pitched.

108. Hal Manders

109. Robert Gerald Miller (1953-1956), and Robert Lane Miller (1973)

110. Clarence Mitchell. His first time up, he hit a line drive which Bill Wambsganss turned into an unassisted triple play. He followed that up by hitting into a double play in his next at-bat, thereby accounting for five outs in two plate appearances.

111. Tom Morgan

112. Joe Coleman (1973)

113. He defeated the Chicago White Sox—the team which originally signed him—by a 4-3 margin, hitting a home run in the process.

114. None. He batted .133, with 82 hits in 616 at-bats in the majors.

The Infield

1. Which Tiger was the first third baseman to win an American League batting title?

2. Who was the Detroit infielder who led off two successive games in 1969 with home runs?

3. Which Tiger infielder of 1920 was the umpire behind the plate in Don Larsen's perfect game in the 1956 World Series?

4. Which infielder was suspended for five days in 1968 following an altercation with Chicago's Tommy John?

5. Name the Detroit infielder who later became manager and general manager of the Angels.

6. Which first baseman batted .343, .326 and .325 in his three full seasons with Detroit?

The Infield — Questions

7. Which Bengal infielder was born in St. Vito Udine, Italy?

8. Can you name the Tiger infielder who once won a $25 bet from Ty Cobb by beating him in a footrace?

9. This infielder of the 1950s and 1960s played half of his 12-year career with the Tigers. He appeared in 1,540 games in the majors, playing only at second base. Can you identify him?

10. This infielder had a 5-for-5 game in 1980, with three singles, a triple and a home run. In addition, he stole a base and started a triple play. Who is he?

11. This shortstop took part in three triple plays in 1911. He also led the AL in walks five times, from 1909 to 1914. Name him.

12. Second baseman Charlie Gehringer, third baseman Marv Owen and shortstop Billy Rogell each played every game of the 1934 season, while first baseman Hank Greenberg missed just one. What was the reason for that missed game?

13. How many RBIs did each of the four infielders garner that season?

The Infield — Questions

14. What nickname did the *Detroit Free Press* give to the 1934 infield?

15. What was infielder Flea Clifton's given name?

16. Who succeeded Charlie Gehringer at second base in 1942?

17. In which sport was former infielder Richie Hebner an All-American in high school?

18. Which former Detroit player jumped to the outlaw Mexican League in 1949?

19. What was Rocky Bridges's given name?

20. What was Charlie Gehringer's uniform number?

21. Can you name the infielder whom *The Sporting News* named as the Most Valuable Player of the American League in 1945?

22. What was his real name?

23. Which Tiger infielder had a brother who was a standout pro football quarterback, and later an announcer?

The Infield — Questions

24. Although he played eight years in the majors, this shortstop hit only 40 home runs in his career. Exactly half of these came with the Tigers in 1962. Name him.

25. Which former Tiger infielder was a nephew of legendary University of Kentucky basketball coach Adolph Rupp?

26. Of what importance is the date of September 9, 1977, in Tiger history?

27. Who was the infield reserve of the 1930s known as "Kid Boots"?

28. This shortstop had only nine hits with Detroit in his brief cup of coffee with the team in 1970, but three of them were homers. Do you remember him?

29. What was the full name of shortstop Topper Rigney?

30. What was Hank Greenberg's uniform number?

31. Which brothers were infield teammates on the 1958 Bengals?

32. On how many pennant-winning teams did George Kell play in his 15-year career?

The Infield — Questions

33. What fielding record did newcomer Ed Brinkman set in 1971?

34. Who was the infielder who appeared in five games on the mound in 1930-1931, compiling an 0-1 mark?

35. Which Detroit utilityman lost a grand slam in 1970 when he passed teammate Don Wert on the basepaths?

36. Which Tiger infielder, while with the Yankees, was the baserunner when Babe Ruth hit his 60th home run in 1927?

37. Who was Detroit's regular second baseman in their maiden American League season, and what is he usually remembered for?

38. Which infielder worked as a gravedigger in the off-season?

39. Which Detroit oldtimer saw his first regular baseball action when he was drafted into the army in World War I?

40. Name the infielder of the 1950s who was born John Michael Paveskovich.

The Infield — Questions

41. Can you name the Bengal infielder whose two-out double in the ninth inning of a game in Oakland broke up a Ken Holtzman no-hitter in 1975?

42. Which infielder slugged six extra-base hits with the bases loaded in 1986 (five doubles and a home run), to lead the majors?

43. Can you name the Tiger infielder who got a hit in his only All-Star at-bat, in 1968, a year in which he finished the regular season with a .200 mark?

44. Which infielder later became President of the Southern League?

45. Which third baseman, when discussing fielding, once said, "When you reach the point when you're too slow to get out of the way, it's time to quit"?

46. How many home runs did infielder Mick Kelleher hit in his 11 years in the majors?

47. What was his explanation for his poor showing of power?

48. Which former Detroit infielder played the third baseman for the New York Knights in the movie *The Natural*?

The Infield — Questions

49. In the American League's first season, 1901, the Tigers had two players who led the league in errors at their respective positions. Can you name them?

50. Prior to joining the Tigers for his last season in the big-leagues, this second baseman was the Giants' player-manager just before John McGraw took over the team. Do you remember him?

51. Name the Tiger infielder who married the daughter of manager Steve O'Neill.

Answers

1. George Kell (1949)

2. Dick McAuliffe

3. Babe Pinelli

4. Dick McAuliffe

5. Fred Haney

6. Dale Alexander

7. Reno Bertoia

8. Jack Warner

9. Frank Bolling

10. Tom Brookens

11. Donie Bush

The Infield — Answers

12. It was played on the Jewish holy day of Yom Kippur

13. Greenberg—139; Gehringer—127; Rogell—100; and Owen—96, for a total of 462 for the infield.

14. "The Battalion of Death"

15. Herman

16. Jimmy Bloodworth

17. Hockey

18. Shortstop Murray Franklin

19. Everett

20. Number 2, since retired by the Tigers

21. Second baseman Eddie Mayo

22. Edward Joseph Mayoski

23. Mark Christman (brother Paul)

24. Chico Fernandez

25. Doug Flynn

The Infield — Answers

26. It was the date on which the keystone duo of Alan Trammell and Lou Whitaker each made his major league debut.

27. Heinie Schuble

28. Ken Szotkiewicz

29. Emory Elmo Rigney

30. Number 5, later retired by the Tigers

31. Frank (2B) and Milt (SS) Bolling

32. None

33. He played 56 consecutive games at shortstop without committing an error.

34. Mark Koenig

35. Dalton Jones (July 9)

36. Mark Koenig

37. Kid Gleason. Gleason later became the manager of the infamous Chicago "Black Sox" squad of 1919.

38. Richie Hebner

39. Infielder Marty McManus

The Infield — Answers

40. Johnny Pesky

41. Tom Veryzer

42. Darnell Coles

43. Don Wert

44. Billy Hitchcock

45. Tom Brookens

46. None

47. "What's one home run? If you hit one, they are just going to want you to hit two."

48. Phil Mankowski

49. Kid Gleason (64 at second base) and Doc Casey (58 at third base)

50. Heinie Smith

51. Skeeter Webb

The Outfield

1. Two Detroit outfielders have recorded fielding percentages of 1.000 for a season. Who are they?

2. The regular Detroit outfield of 1925 compiled a composite batting average of .380. Can you name the men who comprised the trio?

3. Name the Tiger outfielder who hit consecutive grand slams in a 1968 game.

4. What was Bob Molinaro's job in the off-season?

5. This lifetime .311 hitter began his big-league career by hitting .215 in 37 games for Detroit in 1915. Who was this outfielder, who was later dealt to the Browns in exchange for Bill James and Grover Lowdermilk?

The Outfield — Questions

6. This popular Tiger took Hank Greenberg's outfield spot when Hank entered military service in 1941. He then entered the service himself, the next year. Can you name him?

7. Which Detroit flychaser of the 1970s was born in Colon, Panama?

8. This slugging outfielder's claim to trivia fame was that he introduced Joe DiMaggio to Marilyn Monroe. Who is he?

9. How old was outfielder Chuck Hostetler when he finally made it to the majors with the Tigers in 1944?

10. What was Neil Chrisley's given name?

11. Who played the part of Ron LeFlore in *Breakout!*, the movie about his life?

12. Who succeeded Ty Cobb in center field for the Tigers?

13. What "first" did little-known outfielder Frank Huelsman accomplish back in 1904?

14. Which Detroit oldtimer was nicknamed "Kangaroo"?

The Outfield — Questions

15. Can you name the Tiger outfielder who was born in Paris?

16. Name the Detroit outfielder (1940-1941) who played 13 years in the majors, never batting lower than .275.

17. Who hit the third—and last—home run of his brief major league career in the famous 22-inning game between Detroit and New York in 1962?

18. How many players saw action in that contest?

19. Which Tiger outfielder was known for his home run hitting feats on Sundays?

20. How many of his 148 career round-trippers were hit on Sundays?

21. Who was the three-sport star at the University of Michigan who preceded Al Kaline as Detroit's regular right fielder?

22. Which two brothers first reached the majors as outfielders with the 1931 Bengals?

23. What were their given names?

The Outfield — Questions

24. Which Tiger outfielder coached the University of Michigan to the 1962 NCAA baseball title?

25. From which team did the Tigers obtain Charlie Maxwell?

26. Who gave Ty Cobb the nickname "The Georgia Peach"?

27. This former Dodger World Series hero finished his major league career with Detroit in 1960. Can you name him?

28. Recalling his troubled high school days, which outfielder once said, "I took a little English, a little math, some science, a few hubcaps and some wheel covers"?

29. Which rookie flychaser slugged a home run on Opening Day in 1949, then hit two more the second day of the season?

30. This Tiger outfielder later became the Cincinnati Reds' traveling secretary. Can you name him?

31. Where was Sam Crawford born?

32. Can you name the outfielder who homered in each of his first three

The Outfield — Questions

major league games back in 1928, then only once more in his brief, 76-game career?

33. Which current big-league manager ended his eight-year career by appearing in 52 games with the 1963 Bengals?

34. Slugger Willie Horton spent his entire career as an outfielder and designated hitter, except for one game in 1965. What position did he play that day?

35. Which switch-hitter batted a surprising .291 in 1980, and tied infielder Tom Brookens for the team lead in stolen bases?

36. Name the rookie outfielder, born in Palestine, who appeared in 16 games for Detroit in 1953.

37. Who was the outfielder who charged former Tiger pitcher Ed Farmer in a 1980 contest, and was suspended seven games for his actions?

38. How was their feud eventually settled?

39. Outfielder Earl Webb came to Detroit in 1932 in the Dale Alexander deal. What incredible record did he set the year before, while with Boston?

The Outfield — Questions

40. The previous record-holder was another former Tiger. Can you name him?

41. Which Tiger was offered football contracts by both the Chicago Bears and the New York Titans?

42. In how many different seasons have the Tigers had outfields in which each member hit .300?

43. Which was the last trio to accomplish the feat?

44. The 1921 combination of Ty Cobb, Harry Heilmann and Bobby Veach is the only trio in American League history to perform what feat?

45. What was Jo-Jo White's given name?

Answers

1. Mickey Stanley (1968, 1970) and Al Kaline (1971)

2. Right fielder Harry Heilmann (.393), center fielder Ty Cobb (.378) and left fielder Al (Red) Wingo (.370)

3. Jim Northrup

4. He was a blackjack dealer in Las Vegas.

5. Baby Doll Jacobson

6. Pat Mullin

7. Ben Oglivie

8. Gus Zernial

9. He was 40 years old—the oldest non-pitching rookie in major league history.

The Outfield — Answers

10. Barbra

11. Levar Burton

12. Heinie Manush

13. He became the first American Leaguer to play for four different teams in one season (Chicago, Detroit, St. Louis and Washington).

14. Davy Jones

15. Dave Philley (Paris, Texas)

16. Bruce Campbell

17. Purnal Goldy

18. Forty-three—22 by the Tigers and 21 by the Yankees

19. Charlie Maxwell

20. 40 (27 percent)

21. Don Lund

22. Gee and Hub Walker

23. Gerald and Harvey, respectively

24. Don Lund

The Outfield — Answers

25. The Baltimore Orioles (1955)

26. Sportswriter Grantland Rice

27. Sandy Amoros

28. Gates Brown

29. Johnny Groth

30. Paul Campbell

31. Wahoo, Nebraska

32. Paul Easterling

33. Whitey Herzog

34. Third base

35. Ricky Peters

36. Frank Carswell (Palestine, Texas)

37. Al Cowens

38. Cowens and Farmer shook hands at home plate later in the season.

39. He hit a major league record 67 doubles for the Red Sox in 1931.

40. George Burns

The Outfield — Answers

41. Jim Northrup

42. Ten

43. The 1950 group of Hoot Evers, Johnny Groth and Vic Wertz

44. They are the only outfield in which each member drove in more than 100 runs while batting .300 or better (Harry Heilmann—139, .394; Bobby Veach—128, .338; and Ty Cobb—101, .389).

45. Joyner

Records and Firsts

1. In 1974, John Hiller broke the American League record for victories in a season by a relief pitcher. How many games did he win?

2. Who was the Tigers' first free agent acquisition?

3. How did he perform in his first year in a Detroit uniform?

4. In 1982, Lance Parrish broke the AL season mark for home runs by a catcher. How many did he connect for?

5. When Gates Brown set a league record for total pinch hits, he surpassed the mark set by a former Tiger. Can you name this man?

6. What unusual record did Norm Cash tie on June 27, 1963?

Records and Firsts — Questions

7. Which three Tigers have won the AL Rookie of the Year award?

8. Norm Cash batted .361 in 1961 to win the AL batting title. How many times did he reach the .300 mark in his career?

9. The first regular center fielder in Detroit history, this player led the AL in walks in both 1903 and 1904. His total of 74 in 1903 is the lowest ever for an American League leader. Can you name him?

10. In which year did Detroit set the AL record for team batting average for a season?

11. What was their average that year, and in what place did they finish in the standings?

12. Which Tiger holds the all-time record for the highest batting average in All-Star competition (minimum of five games)?

13. Who saved a major league record (since broken) 38 games in 1973?

14. In 1975, Mickey Lolich became baseball's all-time strikeout leader among

Records and Firsts — Questions

lefthanders. Whom did he pass to move into first place?

15. Who later passed Lolich to become the current leader among southpaws?

16. Who set a Detroit all-time mark by garnering 137 walks in 1947?

17. When Ty Cobb stole 96 bases in 1915 to set the Tiger single-season standard, he also set the mark for most times caught stealing in a season. How many times was he thrown out that year?

18. Who was the first Tiger to crack the 20 home run barrier for a season?

19. When Hank Greenberg won the American League RBI title in 1935, the runner-up was Lou Gehrig of the Yankees. How many runs did each drive in?

20. Who is the only Tiger to have homered in his first at-bat in an All-Star Game?

21. What was the longest game that the Tigers have ever been involved in?

22. What was the result of the marathon?

Records and Firsts — Questions

23. Who hurled the final 20 innings for Detroit?

24. The Tigers defeated the Yankees, 10-9, on June 23, 1950. In the game, four Detroit players homered in the fourth inning. Can you name them?

25. Who holds the Tiger season record for the most home runs by a lefthanded batter?

26. Who was the first former Tiger to broadcast their games on radio?

27. Who is the only Tiger to win two consecutive Most Valuable Player awards?

28. Who was the first Tiger to win a Gold Glove award?

29. Which Tiger was twice named the American League's Comeback Player of the Year?

30. What little-known major league record did Milt Wilcox set in 1984?

31. Which three Tiger hurlers have been the winning pitcher in All-Star Games?

Records and Firsts — Questions

32. The 1986 Tigers had six hitters with 20 or more home runs, tying the major league mark. Name them.

33. Who was the first—and last—pitcher to face one-armed outfielder Pete Gray in the majors?

34. In which year did Detroit have three Gold Glove winners for the first time in its history?

35. Who are the only two Tigers to have been elected to ten or more All-Star teams?

36. Who was the first black to play for Detroit?

37. Who is the only pitcher in modern history to have an ERA over 4.00, with more than 3,000 innings pitched?

38. What "first" did outfielder Jimmy Barrett accomplish in 1904?

39. Only one player has ever led the American League in RBIs and stolen bases in the same season. Can you name him?

40. Which two Tigers won *The Sporting News* Rookie Pitcher of the Year

Records and Firsts — Questions

awards in the AL for 1976 and 1977?

41. Who was the first winner of the Tiger of the Year award, as voted by the members of the Detroit Chapter of the BBWA?

42. Who won the first Detroit Rookie of the Year award, as voted by the same group, in 1969?

43. Rookie Rudy York slugged 18 home runs in August of 1937 to set a new record for round-trippers in a month. Whose mark did he break?

44. In 1938, Detroit tied the major league season record for grand slams. How many did the Tigers hit?

45. How many batting crowns did Ty Cobb win?

46. Cobb won those titles over a period of 13 years, failing to win only in 1916. Who took the crown that year, and how did Cobb fare?

47. The last Tiger to lead the AL in triples was a rookie, who did so in 1961. Can you name him?

Records and Firsts — Questions

48. How many times did Hank Greenberg hit two or more homers in a game in 1938?

49. Which AL record did the 1940 Tigers establish in the month of September?

50. Who is the only AL Most Valuable Player to have won the award at two different positions?

51. Which former Detroit pitcher is one of only two 200-game winners in major league history to lose more games than he won?

52. Who was the first unanimous winner of the BBWA Most Valuable Player Award?

53. Who was the first AL switch-hitter to drive in 100 runs in a season?

54. Who hit the first grand slam in Tiger history?

55. Who is Detroit's all-time leader in games played?

56. The first Tiger to get six hits in a game was not Ty Cobb. Can you name the old-timer who accomplished this feat on July 13, 1901?

Records and Firsts — Questions

57. Who was the first player to win Gold Gloves at two positions?

58. Who was the first Detroit hurler to pass the $100,000 mark in salary for a season?

59. How many times in his career did Ty Cobb get five or more hits in a game?

60. Shortly after coming over from Boston in 1952, this first baseman stroked 12 consecutive hits to tie the major league record. Name him.

61. Which pitcher ended this record-tying streak?

62. Name the Detroit relief pitcher who holds the mark for the lowest batting average by a player with at least one career hit.

63. Which Detroit Hall-of-Famer grounded into a record four consecutive double plays in a 1934 game?

64. Who is the only player to have led both the NL and AL in stolen bases in a season?

65. Who was the first Tiger selected in the first amateur draft, held in 1965?

Records and Firsts — Questions

66. Who was the first player to hit a home run out of Tiger Stadium after it was rebuilt in 1938?

67. Who is the only player to hit three balls out of Tiger Stadium in the same season?

68. Which opposing player has cleared the roof of Tiger Stadium the most times?

69. Which former Tiger became the first player in National League history to sign a $100,000 contract?

70. In 1911, this backstop set the AL mark for assists in a season by a catcher. Can you name him?

71. By finishing his career hitting 25 home runs for Pittsburgh in 1947, Hank Greenberg became the first player in history to accomplish what feat?

72. When Ty Cobb was elected to the Hall of Fame, he received the highest percentage of votes ever cast. What was that percentage?

73. In 1922, Harry Heilmann set the major league record for most home runs by a player in an opposing team's park in

Records and Firsts — Questions

one season. How many did he hit in Philadelphia that year?

74. Which rookie pitcher tied a big-league mark in 1986 by recording six putouts in a game?

75. Who was the first big leaguer to hit 40 homers in a season in both the NL and AL?

76. Two of the five players chosen in the first Hall of Fame election both played under a former Detroit manager. Name the players and the manager.

77. Erve (Dutch) Beck was an infielder who finished his brief major league career in 1902 with the Tigers. What noteworthy achievement is he remembered for?

78. Who is the only player in history to lay down two sacrifice bunts in one inning?

79. Who was the first designated hitter in Tiger history?

80. Which former Tiger won 19 games in a season a record four times?

Records and Firsts — Questions

81. Until Lou Brock passed him, Ty Cobb had been baseball's all-time stolen base king. How many did he collect in his career?

82. Who was the first Tiger to slug three home runs in a game?

83. Which Tiger was the first player to appear in an All-Star Game for both leagues?

84. Which other former Tiger was the first man to pitch for both leagues in All-Star Games?

85. How many home runs did Hank Greenberg hit at Briggs Stadium in 1938?

86. The Tigers hold the AL record for consecutive seasons without tossing a no-hitter. How long did they go between gems?

87. Can you name the only Tiger to lead the AL in runs scored, with a total of less than 100?

88. Who is the only Tiger to play in more than 162 games in a season?

Records and Firsts — Questions

89. Which Detroit hurler threw five wild pitches in an August 3, 1987, game against Kansas City to tie the AL record?

90. Which Detroit pitcher set the mark back in 1912?

91. Only two players in history have hit home runs while in their teens and also in their forties. Both played for the Tigers. Can you name them?

Answers

1. 17

2. Former Giant infielder Tito Fuentes

3. He batted .309 in 1977, for the highest mark by a Detroit second baseman since Charlie Gehringer's .313 in 1940.

4. 32

5. Bob (Fats) Fothergill

6. He played an entire game at first base without recording an assist or putout.

7. Harvey Kuenn (1953), Mark Fidrych (1976) and Lou Whitaker (1978)

8. Just that once. His next highest mark was .286, in 1960.

9. Jimmy Barrett

Records and Firsts — Answers

10. 1921

11. .316. They finished in sixth place, 27 games behind the Yankees.

12. Charlie Gehringer (.500, on ten for 20 in six games)

13. John Hiller

14. Warren Spahn

15. Steve Carlton

16. Roy Cullenbine

17. 38

18. Harry Heilmann, with 21 in 1922

19. Greenberg had 170 RBIs, 51 more than Gehrig.

20. Hoot Evers (1948)

21. A 24-inning contest against Philadelphia, on July 21, 1945.

22. It ended in a 1-1 tie.

23. Les Mueller

24. Dizzy Trout, Gerry Priddy, Vic Wertz and Hoot Evers

Records and Firsts — Answers

25. Norm Cash (41 in 1961)

26. Harry Heilmann (1934)

27. Pitcher Hal Newhouser (1944, 1945)

28. Al Kaline (1957)

29. Norm Cash (1965 and 1971)

30. Most games started in a season without a completion—33

31. Tommy Bridges (1939), Virgil Trucks (1949) and Jim Bunning (1957)

32. Darrell Evans (29), Kirk Gibson (28), Lance Parrish (22), Alan Trammell (21), Darnell Coles (20) and Lou Whitaker (20)

33. Hal Newhouser

34. 1983 (Lou Whitaker, Alan Trammell, and Lance Parrish, who also did it in 1984)

35. Al Kaline (18) and Bill Freehan (11)

36. Ozzie Virgil (1958)

37. Earl Whitehill (4.36 in 3,566 innings)

Records and Firsts — Answers

38. He became the first major leaguer to appear in 162 games in a season.

39. Ty Cobb (1907, 1909, and 1911)

40. Mark Fidrych and Dave Rozema

41. Don Wert (1965)

42. Pitcher Mike Kilkenny

43. Babe Ruth's. Ruth clouted 17 homers in September of 1927.

44. Ten, including four by catcher Rudy York

45. A big-league record 12

46. Tris Speaker of Cleveland, with a .386 average. Cobb finished second at .371.

47. Jake Wood

48. A record 11 times

49. They hit at least one home run in 17 consecutive games (September 4 through September 19).

50. Hank Greenberg. He won as a first baseman in 1935 and as a left fielder in 1940.

Records and Firsts — Answers

51. Bobo Newsom (211-222)

52. Hank Greenberg (1935)

53. Billy Rogell (1934)

54. Deacon McGuire (May 18, 1902)

55. Al Kaline (2,834)

56. Doc Nance

57. Al Kaline (right field in 1958 and center field in 1959)

58. Mickey Lolich (1973).

59. A major league record 14 times

60. Walt Dropo

61. Lou Sleater of the Washington Senators. He got Dropo to foul out to the catcher.

62. Fred Gladding (.016 on one for 63)

63. Goose Goslin (April 28)

64. Ron LeFlore (AL in 1978 and NL in 1980)

65. Catcher Gene Lamont

Records and Firsts — Answers

66. Ted Williams (May 4, 1939)

67. Norm Cash in 1962

68. Mickey Mantle of the Yankees (3)

69. Hank Greenberg, with Pittsburgh, in 1947

70. Oscar Stanage

71. He was the first player to hit 20 or more homers in a season in both leagues.

72. 98.2% (222 of 226)

73. Ten of his 21 homers

74. Eric King

75. Darrell Evans (NL in 1973, AL in 1985)

76. Honus Wagner and Babe Ruth both played for Ed Barrow, Wagner while with Paterson of the Atlantic League in 1896, and Ruth with the Red Sox in 1918-1919.

77. While with Cleveland in 1901, he hit the first home run in the history of the American League.

Records and Firsts — Answers

78. Al Benton (August 6, 1941)

79. Gates Brown (1973)

80. Jim Bunning (1962 with Detroit; 1964, 1965 and 1966 with Philadelphia)

81. 892

82. Ty Cobb (May 5, 1925)

83. Pitcher Schoolboy Rowe

84. Jim Bunning. Rowe's 1947 appearance was as a pinch-hitter.

85. Thirty-nine, the most ever hit in one ballpark in a single season

86. Thirty-nine years. George Mullin threw one on July 4, 1912, and Virgil Trucks the next, on May 15, 1952.

87. Dick McAuliffe (95 in 1968)

88. Rocky Colavito (163 in 1961)

89. Jack Morris

90. Charles Wheatley

91. Ty Cobb and Rusty Staub

Photographs

1. Ty Cobb is second on the all-time triples list. How many three-baggers did he hit, and who is the only player to have hit more?

Photographs—Questions

2. This Hall-of-Famer smacked 200 hits in only his second full season in the majors, but never again reached the coveted mark in 19 additional years. Who is he?

Photographs—Questions

3. Hall-of-Fame backstop Mickey Cochrane caught 1,451 games in the majors. Only once, in 1932, did he play a different position. Where did he play?

Photographs—Questions

4. Can you name this Tigers star, who lost his life by drowning in October of 1986?

162

Photographs—Questions

5. Better known for his slugging, this outfielder had a 1-0 record with a 0.00 ERA in two appearances on the mound in his big-league career. Name him.

Photographs—Questions

6. How many division titles has Sparky Anderson won in his 18 years as a manager in the big leagues (through 1987)?

Photographs—Questions

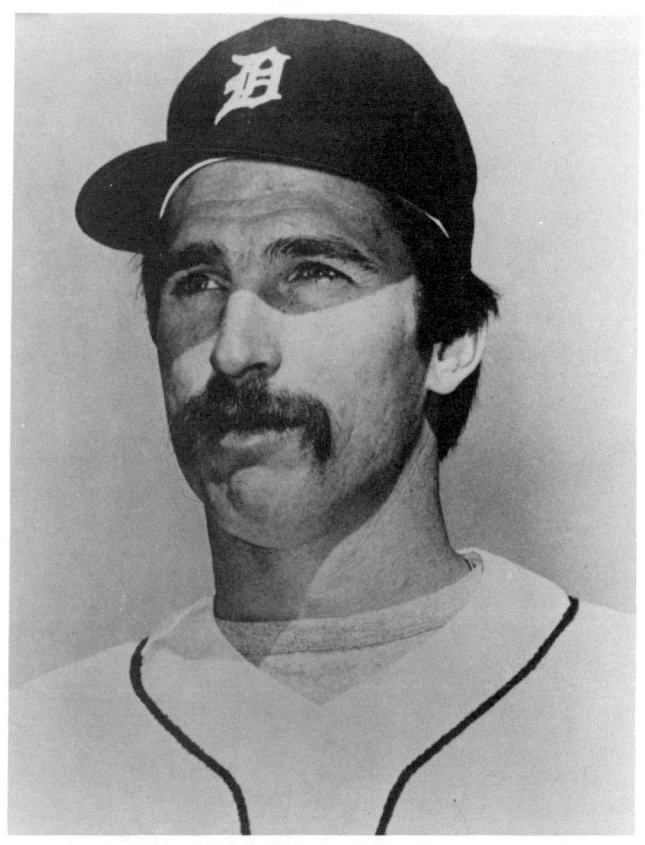

7. Jack Morris has had only one losing year in 11 big-league seasons. What was the year, and what was his record?

Photographs—Questions

8. Where was second baseman Lou Whitaker born?

Photographs—Questions

9. Alan Trammell stole 21 bases in 1987. How many times was he caught stealing that year?

Photographs—Questions

10. This player has reached double figures in home runs in each of the past 17 seasons (through 1987). Can you name him?

Answers

1. 297; Cobb's former teammate Sam Crawford leads the all-time list with 312.

2. Al Kaline

3. In the outfield for Philadelphia

4. Norm Cash

5. Rocky Colavito

6. 7 (5 with Cincinnati—1970, '72, '73, '75, '76; and 2 with Detroit—1984, 1987)

7. 3-5

Photographs—Answers

8. Brooklyn, New York

9. Only twice, good for a success rate of 91 percent

10. Darrell Evans

Miscellaneous — Questions

1. This former Tiger hit an incredible eight home runs in a minor league game for Corsicana of the Texas League in 1905. Can you name him?

2. Which Tiger once turned down a $100,000 contract because he didn't think he was worth the money?

3. Why did Gee and Hub Walker sign contracts with Detroit when New York offered them more money?

4. Which Detroit slugger was struck out by Ted Williams in Williams's only pitching appearance in the majors?

5. What was Bruce Kimm best known for in his two years with Detroit (1976-1977)?

6. In December of 1975, the Tigers and

Miscellaneous — Questions

Astros completed a seven-player deal which included a pair of players (one a pitcher and one an outfielder) with the same surname. Can you name them?

7. Likewise, a 1937 deal between the Tigers and White Sox involved an exchange of two outfielders with the same surname. Who were they?

8. Whom did Ty Cobb call "the only man in the game I can't scare"?

9. Which cousins played for the Tigers in the 1970s?

10. What is the Fred Hutchinson award given for?

11. This Detroit reliever attended Dartmouth College, and was an All-American swimmer in high school. Can you name him?

12. Which Detroit pitcher was born in Coleman, Michigan, and was a teammate of Joe Coleman on the Tigers in 1974, 1975 and 1976?

13. Which former Detroit player hit his only big-league homer off of his brother?

Miscellaneous — Questions

14. The first relief pitcher to win a Cy Young award began his major league career with the Tigers in 1967. Can you name him?

15. Can you name the Tiger pitcher of the early 1900s who was born in Gothenburg, Sweden?

16. Before finishing out his career with Detroit in 1960, this righthander pitched six years with the Giants. He was the winner of the game in which Willie Mays made his big-league debut in 1951. Who is he?

17. Which Detroit hurler won the decathlon in the 1927 Penn Relays?

18. Which Tiger was born in a city whose name was the same as his?

19. Who is the only Tiger to have two consecutive-game streaks of 500 or more games to his credit?

20. Finishing out his big-league career with the Tigers in 1968, this player was the last Boston Brave still active in the majors. Name him.

21. Which Hall-of-Famer is the father-in-law of Denny McLain?

Miscellaneous — Questions

22. What Detroit personality wrote *The Game for All America*?

23. Former Tiger Earl Averill homered in his first major league at-bat, while with Cleveland in 1929. Who was the Detroit hurler who surrendered the blast?

24. Which Detroit rookie of 1987 named The Dead Milkmen as his favorite rock group?

25. Which Tiger once worked as a bodyguard for rock star Tina Turner?

26. Can you name the Tiger first baseman of the 1920s who is buried in Arlington National Cemetery?

27. Which baseball immortal was a distant relative of former Tiger hurler Jack Billingham?

28. Name the Detroit sportscaster who once said, "Sparky (Anderson) came here two years ago promising to build a team in his own image, and now the club is looking for small, white-haired infielders with .212 batting averages"?

29. In which two seasons did Tiger teams have 100 or more victories, yet fail to win the pennant?

Miscellaneous — Questions

30. Which are the only three major league franchises to average over 1,000,000 in home attendance each year of their existence?

31. Which member of the infamous Chicago "Black Sox" began his major league career with Detroit in 1905?

32. Name two other "Black Sox" players who also made their big-league debuts with the Tigers.

33. Frank Lary's brother, Yale, was also known to Detroit sports fans. What team did he play for?

34. Which Tiger pitcher later became a golf pro, and once held the record for the longest hole-in-one ever hit (427 yards)?

35. Name the Detroit reserve catcher who later earned fame as a batting coach with the Kansas City Royals.

36. Which former Tiger catcher was born in Dublin, Ireland?

37. Only one Tiger pitcher has ever won a Gold Glove. Can you name him?

Miscellaneous — Questions

38. Which former Detroit hurler recorded the first win in Seattle Mariner history?

39. What was Rick Leach's best sport in college?

40. Name two former Detroit players whose first names contain all five vowels.

41. In 1983, this Detroit hurler became the first player to ever have his salary reduced after arbitration. Name him.

42. Prior to striking out five consecutive batters in the 1934 All-Star Game, Carl Hubbell faced a Tiger, and former Tiger, to start the game. Who were they, and how did they fare against "King Carl"?

43. Only one player in history has ever hit for the cycle on Opening Day. Can you name this Tiger?

44. Which former Tiger made the final out of the All-Star Game three different times?

45. In which two seasons have the Tigers put together 14-game winning streaks?

Miscellaneous — Questions

46. Name the Detroit broadcaster who entered the Hall of Fame in 1981 as a winner of the Ford Frick award.

47. Which Detroit pitcher was known as "The Yankee Killer"?

48. Which two Hall-of-Famers broadcast Tiger games on television?

49. The flagpole in center field at Tiger Stadium is the highest outfield obstacle ever in play in any big league stadium. How high is it?

50. Browns' pitcher John Whitehead was credited with only one win in 1940, the last of his major league career. What was noteworthy about it?

51. What tragic event in Ty Cobb's life occurred shortly before he was brought up by the Tigers in 1905?

52. What unusual infraction was catcher Mike Heath called for in the Tigers' May 12, 1987, game against California?

53. What was Mark Fidrych's explanation when asked why he didn't have an agent?

Miscellaneous — Questions

54. Which two former Tigers were both nicknamed "The Earl of Snohomish"?

55. Which Tiger catcher from the early days of the American League was born in Berlin, Germany?

56. Who was the first major league player to have a candy bar named after him?

57. Ty Cobb stroked his 4,000th hit while a member of the Philadelphia Athletics. Who was the Detroit pitcher who surrendered the historic safety?

58. Which former Tiger is currently a member of Congress, representing the state of Kentucky?

59. Which Tiger pitcher made his debut on May 2, 1939, the same day that Lou Gehrig's 2,130 consecutive game playing streak ended?

60. Which future Tiger was born on that same day?

61. Has anyone ever hurled a perfect game against the Tigers?

62. Who was the losing pitcher for the Bengals that day?

63. Which Tiger got the first base hit that

Miscellaneous — Questions

Walter Johnson ever surrendered in the majors?

64. Which Hall-of-Famer was named after catcher Mickey Cochrane?

65. Name the Tiger first baseman whose father was a jockey who finished second in the 1912 Kentucky Derby.

66. Which Tiger catcher is the author of *Behind the Mask*?

67. Who is the former Tiger pitcher who went on to become the mayor of Ney, Ohio?

68. Who was known as "The Mechanical Man"?

69. This former Tiger is the only man to appear in all 19 World Series games played by the Washington Senators. Can you name him?

70. Which Detroit hurler (1929-1933) reputedly had the smallest feet of any player in big-league history?

71. Which former Tiger was appointed special assistant to Commissioner Happy Chandler in 1945?

72. Which Tiger pitcher became the

Miscellaneous — Questions

Information and Services Coach for the Chicago Cubs in 1971?

73. The daughter of which Tiger hurler is in the LPGA Hall of Fame?

74. Which Tiger did columnist Jim Murray call, "Gulliver in a Baseball Suit"?

75. The Tigers are the only major league club with a winning record in each season of the 1980s. When was the last year that the team fell below .500?

76. Two of the streets bordering Tiger Stadium were Cherry Street and National Avenue. What are they now known as?

77. What does former Met Ed Kranepool have in common with Hank Greenberg?

78. Which former Tiger was the first rookie in National League history to hit three homers in one game?

79. Which Tiger star was nicknamed "Boogie" by his parents due to his unsteadiness afoot when learning how to walk?

80. Whose alleged "breakfast of cham-

Miscellaneous — Questions

pions" consisted of two fried eggs and a bottle of beer?

81. Which former Tiger slugger is a gourmet chef, with his own restaurant in New York City?

82. This former football teammate of George Gipp, under Knute Rockne at Notre Dame, was also a teammate of Red Grange in the NFL. Playing five games with Detroit in 1922, he batted 1.000, with a hit in his only big-league at-bat. Name him.

83. Who was the Michigan State quarterback who played six years in the AFL, and caught one game for the Tigers in 1957?

84. Name the former Tiger who preceded Miller Huggins as manager of the New York Yankees in 1915-1917.

85. Can you name the Tiger who pinch-hit, played the outfield, then pitched, all in the same game in 1964?

86. Who is the only lefthanded batter in history to play an entire season of 150 or more games without grounding into a double play?

87. This Detroit catcher played baseball,

Miscellaneous — Questions

football and basketball in high school, and set a state record in the javelin. Can you name him?

88. Which former Tiger went on to become the first player ever ejected from a World Series game?

89. What do former Ownie Carroll, Gene Desautels and Jimmy Shevlin have in common?

90. Who was reputed to be the first player to come to the plate swinging three bats so as to make the bat he was going to use feel lighter?

91. Can you name the native of Zborov, Czechoslovakia, who appeared in three games for the 1952 Bengals, going 0-for-2 as a pinch-hitter?

92. Which brother combination played for Detroit back in 1912?

93. What positions did the following Tigers play in their initial pro seasons: Mike Heath, Chet Lemon, Lance Parrish?

94. What is Rusty Staub's given name?

95. Mickey Cochrane made his major league debut with the Athletics on

Miscellaneous — Questions

April 14, 1925. Which other Hall-of-Famer made his debut in the same game?

96. Where is Tigertown, the Tigers' spring training base, located?

97. Where did the Bengals train prior to moving to Lakeland?

Answers

1. Nig Clarke

2. Al Kaline (1971)

3. Their mother, a true southerner, would not let her sons sign with a team called the Yankees.

4. Rudy York (August 24, 1940)

5. He was Mark Fidrych's "personal" catcher.

6. Outfielder Leon Roberts, who went to Houston, and pitcher Dave Roberts, who came to Detroit

7. Dixie Walker, who came to Detroit, and Gee Walker, who went to Chicago

8. Pittsburgh's Honus Wagner

Miscellaneous — Answers

9. Pitcher Ike Brookens and infielder Tom Brookens

10. It is awarded annually to the major league player who overcomes a form of adversity, and exemplifies the character and fighting spirit demonstrated by former Tiger hurler Hutchinson.

11. Chuck Seelbach

12. Vern Ruhle

13. Joe Niekro, off brother Phil in 1976

14. Mike Marshall

15. Eric Erickson

16. George Spencer

17. Vern Kennedy

18. Slim Love, from Love, Missouri

19. Charlie Gehringer (511 and 504)

20. Eddie Mathews

21. Lou Boudreau

22. Broadcaster Ernie Harwell

Miscellaneous — Answers

23. Earl Whitehill

24. Jim Walewander

25. Lance Parrish

26. Lu Blue

27. Christy Mathewson

28. Al Ackerman

29. In 1915, when Detroit finished at 100-54, 2½ games behind Boston, and in 1961, when they finished at 101-61, eight games behind the Yankees

30. Detroit, the New York Yankees and the Brooklyn/Los Angeles Dodgers

31. Eddie Cicotte

32. Lefty Williams, and Fred McMullin

33. He was a punter for the Detroit Lions of the NFL.

34. Lou Kretlow

35. Charlie Lau

36. Jimmy Archer

37. Frank Lary (1961)

Miscellaneous — Answers

38. Bill Laxton (1977)

39. Football. He was an All-American quarterback at the University of Michigan.

40. Aurelio Lopez and Aurelio Rodriguez

41. Aurelio Lopez

42. Charlie Gehringer opened up with a single, and former Tiger Heinie Manush followed with a walk. Hubbell then proceeded to fan Babe Ruth, Lou Gehrig, Jimmie Foxx, Al Simmons and Joe Cronin—in order.

43. Gee Walker (April 20, 1937)

44. Harvey Kuenn (1956, 1959 and 1960)

45. 1909 and 1934

46. Ernie Harwell

47. Frank Lary

48. Al Kaline and George Kell

49. It stands 125 feet tall.

50. It was a six-inning no-hitter against the Tigers, on August 5.

Miscellaneous — Answers

58. Jim Bunning

59. Fred Hutchinson

60. Gates Brown

51. His father was accidentally shot and killed by his mother, who apparently thought he was a burglar trying to break into their home.

52. After blocking a Dan Petry pitch in the dirt, Heath scooped the ball up with his mask. Angel manager Gene Mauch claimed this was a violation of the rule which forbids a player from deliberately obstructing a thrown ball with any part of the uniform. Umpire Durwood Merrill agreed, and awarded both California runners two bases. The Tigers eventually won the game, 15-2.

53. "Why should I give somebody 10 percent when I do all the work"?

54. Earl Averill and Earl Torgeson, both from Snohomish, Washington

55. Fritz Buelow

56. Ty Cobb

57. Sam Gibson (July 19, 1927)

Miscellaneous — Answers

61. Yes, Charlie Robertson of Chicago, on April 30, 1922

62. Herman Pillette

63. Ty Cobb

64. Mickey Mantle

65. Ferris Fain

66. Bill Freehan

67. Ned Garver

68. Charlie Gehringer

69. Goose Goslin

70. Art Herring (size 3)

71. Catcher Muddy Ruel

72. Hank Aguirre

73. George Suggs (father of golfing great Louise Suggs)

74. Frank Howard

75. 1977 (74-88, .457)

76. Kaline Drive and Cochrane Avenue, respectively

Miscellaneous — Answers

77. Both attended James Monroe High School in the Bronx, New York.

78. Eddie Mathews, with Milwaukee, on September 27, 1952.

79. Willie Horton

80. Boots Poffenberger's

81. Rusty Staub

82. Johnny Mohardt

83. Tom Yewcic

84. Wild Bill Donovan

85. Willie Smith

86. Dick McAuliffe (1968)

87. Matt Batts

88. Hall-of-Famer Heinie Manush, while with Washington in 1933

89. Each attended Holy Cross College.

90. Ty Cobb

91. Carl Linhart

92. Eddie and Jack Onslow

Miscellaneous — Answers

93. Heath—SS, 2B, and 3B at Johnson City in 1973; Lemon—SS, and 3B at Coos Bay in 1972; and Parrish—3B, and OF at Bristol in 1974

94. Daniel

95. Lefty Grove

96. Lakeland, Florida

97. San Antonio, Texas